blue
rider
press

Will Not Attend

Will Not Attend

LIVELY STORIES OF DETACHMENT AND ISOLATION

Adam Resnick

BLUE RIDER PRESS

a member of Penguin Group (USA)

New York

blue
rider
press

Published by the Penguin Group
Penguin Group (USA) LLC
375 Hudson Street
New York, New York 10014

USA · Canada · UK · Ireland · Australia
New Zealand · India · South Africa · China

penguin.com
A Penguin Random House Company

Library of Congress Cataloging-in-Publication Data

Resnick, Adam.
[Essays. Selections]
Will not attend: lively stories of detachment and isolation / Adam Resnick.
p.   cm.
ISBN 978-0-399-16038-7
1. Resnick, Adam.   2. Television writers—United States—Biography.
3. Screenwriters—United States—Biography.   I. Title.
PN1992.4.R48A3   2014   2013050271
812'.6—dc23
[B]

Printed in the United States of America
1   3   5   7   9   10   8   6   4   2

Book design by Michelle McMillian

For my parents

Contents

"Come on in and have a breakfast sandwich, sir. It'll put a smile on your face. You can't walk around looking that angry all the time."

—CALLED OUT TO ME BY A CHEERFUL BLACK WOMAN
HAWKING EGG SANDWICHES OUTSIDE
A DELI ON FORTY-EIGHTH AND SEVENTH

An Easter Story

There was Patrick Swope's eighth birthday party, a sleepover at Jeff Kay's, and a backyard carnival for muscular dystrophy at Tony Geisinger's—a flurry of affairs over a two-week period that pretty much sealed my fate. The condensed timing of these events and my refusal to attend every one of them highlighted a pattern of behavior that my mother had long been concerned about: I didn't like to socialize with other kids. By the time an invitation arrived for an Easter party at Eddie Hoke's, I knew I was screwed. She told me in no uncertain terms I'd be going and that was that. "You don't want to get a reputation as a kook," she said. "The neighborhood already has Greg Peifer." Greg Peifer was an older boy who lived up the street, a schizophrenic who had a habit of leaving bottle caps filled with urine in people's mailboxes, sometimes accompanied by a piece of Scripture.

While I've never claimed to be one of those happy, well-adjusted types, I was certainly no Greg Peifer. I simply had an aversion to social interaction with my peers. Sure, I had a few friends whose company I enjoyed in measured doses, but in general I found kids to be off-putting, especially in second grade. Boys were obviously the worst. I couldn't stand the way they shouted all the time, hated their cretinous obsession with weaponry and construction vehicles, and was never a fan of the whole make-a-fart-sound-with-your-armpit thing. Sadly, I had little choice in the matter; it was an experience mandated by the state. What I really resented, though, was being roped into hanging around kids beyond the required hours of school. Everything in their homes nauseated me; the furniture, the pets, the fucking boat in the garage, and the way their moms tossed out words like "hamper," "pantry," and "coverlet." Their milk was made from powder and the toilet water was blue. Assholes! It's all burned into my brain—from Rob Ecker's dad cutting his birthday cake with a pocketknife to the Folletts' use of baby food jars as drinking glasses. Christ, Andy Boyle's grandmother actually *lived* with him. Grim.

The day of the Easter party closed in like a lurking

predator, and I began feeling more trapped by the minute. But my wheels were turning. Abdominal deception had freed me from more childhood obligations than I can remember. It got me out of Sunday school, saved me from visiting my aunt Shirley in Dillsburg, and allowed me to dodge *Hello, Dolly!* at the Hershey Theatre. Unfortunately, the stomachache gag had grown shopworn with the old lady and could no longer be relied on. I had roughly a week to build some credibility.

I eased into it, complaining of mild queasiness on Monday after school. By Tuesday morning I spoke of an unusual ringing in my ears, which I likened to sleigh bells. Wednesday I tripped over the dog, claiming I thought it was a spot on the rug. At dinner on Thursday I stared at my hand for ten minutes before uttering in a flat voice, "Where is Grandpa buried?" By the time I shuffled out the door Friday morning, blowing my nose like a baggy-pants comic in a doctor sketch, my mother was applauding from the front porch. "Bravo!" she called out. "Encore! Encore!" I sharply told her that if she didn't believe I was sick, the school nurse would. That got her attention—if the nurse confirmed an illness, especially of a mental variety, it would reflect badly on her parenting skills. So we split the difference and she gave me a note to stay in at recess. In other words, she blinked. She opened her mind to the possibility that perhaps I really wasn't feeling well. All I had to do now was feign a seizure on Saturday and it was a done deal. The Hoke Easter party would have to muddle through without me.

Karen Milojevich had been the object of my fascination since kindergarten. She was a cute little knock-kneed girl with a crooked smile and copper-colored hair usually kept in uneven braids, one fatter than the other. Like me, she was as pale as a lightbulb, indicating an aversion to fresh air and the outdoors. But her magnificence didn't end there. She rarely interacted with the other kids and often appeared lost in her own thoughts. One time, from a distance, I observed her standing alone by a tree in the playground. Her lips were moving, mouthing words, but no one was there.

She was perfection.

And now, for the first time, we were alone: sitting two rows away from each other in an empty classroom during recess. She, retaking a quiz on long vowels, and me, captivated by the ink-stained rubber band that held her pigtail (the fat one).

Karen finished the exam and placed her pencil on the desk. "That was easy," she offered cheerfully with a half glance in my direction. I swiftly replied, "Yeah, sometimes the hardest tests are the easiest," which didn't really track, but sounded supportive. She stared out the window.

"Too bad you had to miss recess," I threw out.

She considered this for a beat, and responded wistfully, "Yes, but . . . recess can be so stupid sometimes."

I decided to take her point a step further, stating bluntly, "I hate the sound of children playing."

Even from the back of her head I could make out that enchanting cockeyed smile. I nearly fell out of my chair when she announced she'd been invited to Eddie Hoke's Easter party on Sunday. A weary sigh followed and she turned to me.

"Are you going?"

When my mother observed me in fine health and high spirits, she was disturbed. It was the day before the party—why wasn't I moping? Where was my pre-party bitterness? Shouldn't I be complaining of chest pains or something? When I informed her of my desire to arrive at Eddie's house extra early so I wouldn't "miss out on any of the fun," she sat me down for a series of questions: Did I get clocked by a baseball at school? Had I been fooling around with turpentine when the painters were here? Was I constipated? With her neurological and gastrointestinal checklist complete, she appeared satisfied—hopeful even. Moments later, I overheard her tell my father in a low but excited voice, "I think he's finally turned the corner . . . mentally." He advised her not to get her hopes up.

The Hoke affair turned out to be pretty much as advertised—a couple of picnic tables in the backyard with baloney sandwiches, lime Kool-Aid, and oily potato chips shimmering in the sun. An inflated pink bunny hung from a nearby tree as if it had been lynched. None of the bleak details mattered, though, because Karen was there. She was wearing a gingham dress with patches of yellow flowers and black patent leather shoes. The braids were gone, in favor of a lopsided ponytail. As usual, she seemed shy and uncomfortable around the other kids, but I didn't rush over to her. I wanted everything to happen naturally.

Before long, I found myself participating in relay races and other infantile theatrics that were an insult to my intelligence. Karen ran like an awkward bird, which I found delightful. At one point, Roger Boyce, who was flailing his arms like a spaz, ran his fat ass into a tree and started bawling. I looked over at Karen, who had her hand over her mouth, trying not to laugh. She saw me and nodded her head, as if to say, "Wasn't that great? Wouldn't it have been even better if he'd broken his neck?" What a gal, this Karen Milojevich!

At long last, it was time for the perfunctory egg hunt. Mr. Hoke, in full Rockefeller mode, grandly announced that one of the plastic eggs contained a dollar bill. Then he counted down from ten and fired a starter pistol into the air. Kids shrieked and scattered in all directions. I just stood there for a moment, stunned. *Was the goddamn gun really necessary?* I thought. My fucking ears were ringing.

Then I noticed Karen. She was waiting for me! Soon, we were at each other's side, searching for eggs and laughing about how stupid it all was. We were united in our mutual disgust for everything other kids enjoyed. I suggested we do our best to find the dollar bill, merely to ruin things for everyone else. She liked the idea. And why wouldn't she? She'd laughed at Roger Boyce.

Mr. and Mrs. Hoke stood in the yard, smiling and holding hands as Mr. Hoke urged us onward: "Keep looking! It could be *anywhere*! Put your thinking caps on!" I wanted to ask him where his thinking cap was when he'd blown my eardrums out. I suggested to Karen that we search inside the house, leaving the others to frisk bushes and step in dachshund shit. There was something about the way Mr. Hoke had said "It could be *anywhere*" that made me think the backyard was a ruse. We had a wise guy on our hands.

Inside the Hoke living room (which smelled like cabbage and Brylcreem), I immediately impressed Karen by finding an egg under the key cover on the piano. It contained only a couple of fuck-you jellybeans, but I was now more emboldened than ever. We discovered a few more duds under some cushions, and another one inside the refrigerator wedged between an open bowl of potato salad and a bottle of insulin. That cost us a few seconds as I dry-heaved over the sink.

After a thorough sweep of the upstairs bedrooms and a

hallway linen closet lined with cat hair, we entered Mr. Hoke's office. Mr. Hoke owned a furniture store in downtown Harrisburg, and the room was cluttered with junk like fabric samples and lamp brochures. The walls were dotted with family photos and a few shots of Mr. Hoke standing outside his store next to an old guy who looked like Groucho Marx.

We waded in.

His desk yielded nothing. The bookshelf was a bust. And the only things under the sofa were a broken domino and a dead Milk-Bone. Then I saw the filing cabinet. It was in the corner of the room behind a tall chair, practically unnoticeable. I was suddenly consumed with an overpowering sense of belief, as if I had been guided to this very spot. I *knew* the egg was in there. It was waiting for Karen and me—a symbolic confirmation of our eternal union. I was so excited I gave her a quick impulsive hug. It lasted no more than two seconds, but she didn't resist. It was our planet now.

Operating on instinct, I opened the bottom drawer marked INVOICES. The folders inside were jammed tightly together and made a clacking sound against the metal frame, as if to say, "Welcome, pal!" By now, my confidence had Karen giggling with anticipation. She even rested her hand on my shoulder for a moment. I reached in to pull out a particularly thick file to see if the egg was underneath it, but it wouldn't budge. Instead, my fingers inadvertently latched onto a loose document. It slid out with only minor resistance and was now in my hand. It wasn't an invoice though. Or a brochure, or a card of fabric samples.

It was a photograph of a woman sucking off a horse.

Everything stopped. Over and over I tried to get myself to see something different, but the image remained true; as valid as the sound of Karen's measured breathing behind my back. I turned around. She was gazing at the photograph with locked eyes, as if forced to contemplate something she'd always dreaded. Wordlessly, I quickly jammed the picture back in the filing cabinet. As I shut the drawer, I became aware of movement in the room. I peered over my shoulder just in time to catch a glimpse of Karen's white ankle sock passing through the doorframe. Cheers erupted from outside. Groucho looked down at me, smirking. Someone had found the egg.

Fucking parties.

I was still in a fog the next morning. Even as I tried to eat my cereal, the air around me felt damp and murky. It had not been a dream: for a brief moment, on the anniversary of Christ's resurrection, I held in my hand a photograph of a woman fellating a horse. A lone grungy piece of a mysterious puzzle. (Well, there was also Donald Whitman's oft-told joke about a guy named Johnny Fuckerfaster, but that was more idiotic than disturbing.) What other secrets did adults have? What terrible things awaited me when I grew up? Just when I thought it couldn't get any worse than elementary school, *this*. There was only one person capable of understanding what I was feeling—someone who needed me right now as badly as I needed her. But in class that Monday, the day after the party, Karen Milojevich would not look at me. She would not catch my glance nor allow me to enter her line of sight. Not at recess, not in the cafeteria or the art room. For some incomprehensible reason, she appeared to be blaming me for what had occurred at Eddie Hoke's house. This marked the first in a long line of personal experiences I would come to recognize as "the story of my life."

June came quickly that year, and on the last day of school, Karen seemed to vanish into the clouds. There were no good-byes. No explanations or tearful confessions. She was just gone. Not one word had passed between us since the Easter party.

I now viewed my life in two segments: before the horse picture and after. The more I tried to forget the image, the more I obsessed over it. It was a bell that could not be un-rung, and I fixated on every horrific detail: the muddy field, the chubby woman with her bare knees lodged in the muck, and the weary look on the horse's face as he gazed slightly off camera. What was he thinking? Was he staring down some distant road, hoping to see a cop? Or perhaps just conjuring the memory of a gentle mare he'd known in happier times.

The summer groaned forward like a mail truck overloaded with disturbing photographs from Denmark. Each day felt hotter and longer than the one before, and the sun grew blinding. I kept to myself mostly, avoiding the neighborhood kids. Occasionally I made an appearance at the township pool, where I'd find an empty corner and float facedown until I was obliged to flip over and breathe. Sometimes I found myself taking long bike rides and losing all sense of aware-ness. One day, I rode the whole way from the lumberyard to Goose Valley Road in a hailstorm and barely noticed. I re-member passing the Hokes' house one afternoon and seeing Eddie and Mr. Hoke playing catch in the front yard. They both waved to me, and Mr. Hoke called out, "Hey, there, stranger! Long time, no see!" I kept pedaling. Poor sweet dumb Eddie. If he only knew the old man like I did.

Sleep came hard during those months. Always, my mind drifted to Karen. Rumor had it she'd gone away to camp in the Poconos. It was too impossible to consider—camp in-volved activities and group interaction. Her parents must have slipped her some knockout drops and stuffed her into the trunk. Hours later, she probably woke up on a tennis court. If only I had been there to save her.

August died a hot miserable death, giving way to September, which proved to be equally hot and miserable. The doors of James Buchanan Elementary School creaked open like a giant brick oven, and once again I was surrounded by ape-children who would grow up to do things like name schools after shitty presidents. The classroom slowly filled with the usual suspects, who seemed to have changed very little since second grade. Roger Boyce was wearing a red bow tie, looking like a bloated ventriloquist dummy. He was already kissing Miss Oberholtzer's ass, who sat behind her desk, silent and grim-faced, like some ancient hysterectomied toad. I quickly grabbed a prime seat in the back row.

It was there I waited for her.

Karen was the last student to enter the room, and my heart immediately sank when I saw her: she looked tanned and happy. I watched in horror as she eagerly chatted with other kids about her summer. Appalling words like "tire swing" and "lake" tumbled out of her mouth. My worst fears had been realized: she was now one of them. I waited, praying she'd look my way, and when she finally did (by accident), she acknowledged me with a courteous nod, as if I were someone she had vaguely known once. The profound connection we had shared last Easter was gone. I wanted to stab myself, but the little red scissors in my desk had rounded edges.

As fate would have it, the first birthday party of third

grade turned out to be Karen's, in October. To my knowledge, it was the first time she'd ever held such an event. The entire class was invited; I was just part of the head count. Still, I had never wanted to attend anything more in my life. I'd already decided it would be there that I'd confront her about last spring and what we'd seen at Eddie Hoke's house. The photograph had put us both under some kind of spell, like characters in a Grimms' fairy tale, and I needed to save her as much as I needed to save myself.

The party was noisy and crowded, and my plan seemed doomed from the start. I was alone in the kitchen, hiding from musical chairs, when the moment unexpectedly arrived. Karen walked in, giggling to herself about something, and opened the refrigerator. When she closed the door, she saw me lurking in the back corner of the room next to the cat bowls.

"Can I talk to you?" I said.

She stood motionless, holding a bottle of Wink soda. After a moment, she shrugged her shoulders. *Finally! We were communicating again.* I had to choose my next words very carefully. I had to take her back in time, before everything had changed, before we saw what we saw. Did I detect a hint of that old crooked smile creeping across her face?

"Kaaaren! Time to open presents!" It was the spiky voice of her grandmother calling from the living room. There was a brief stillness in the kitchen. Karen regarded me for a moment with a faint look of pity, shrugged her shoulders again, and hurried out.

As a chorus of "oohs" and "ahhs" filled the air, scraps of wrapping paper fluttered aimlessly through the Milojevich living room like dying birds. The final present was the largest, and Karen tore into it fiercely, shredding the *Peanuts*-themed paper until only a portion of Violet's scalp remained. Her eyes grew wide, and the squeal she emitted was pure and joyful. She lifted herself from the floor and raised the box high in the air, like Moses revealing the tablets. Behold! *Barbie and Her Magic Horse, "Dancer"*!

My gaze fell on her smile. It was perfect, without a trace of imbalance. Then up the stairs she went with her treasure, trailed by a parade of eight-year-old girls in crinkly dresses.

I was left alone with the boys. David Kitmer was smearing icing under his nose, pretending it was snot. Other kids followed suit. Karen's grandmother lit up a Kent. And the safety switch in my head finally tripped off, suspending electrical activity in my brain. That would be my present—the greatest gift of all.

Many years later, when I was in ninth grade, the Hokes relocated to San Diego. By then, I rarely thought about Karen

Milojevich or that long-ago Easter party. The whole matter had been nicely tucked away in the back of my mind, a little annuity guaranteed to fuck me up in ways I'd never be able to identify. So I was surprised by the incredible buoyancy I felt as I watched the moving van pull out of the neighborhood. It was in there somewhere probably, riding along in a box marked PAPERWORK: JERRY'S OFFICE—DO NOT OPEN. Maybe when the truck crossed the Arizona border, that peculiar woman would finally stop sucking—just long enough for the horse to kick his way out and run into the desert.

Booker's a Nice Guy

My mother wanted me and my brother Mike out of the house. It was a typical Sunday, when the toll of having six children— all boys—brought her nervous system to the brink of collapse. Though she was generally a saint in every regard, you could always tell when her mood had shifted and "Bad Joyce" ar- rived. Doors and cupboards would begin to slam, and her soft voice would be replaced by something a good deal sharper.

On this particular morning, she was set off by what I'd intended as a simple rhetorical question: "Aw, who ate all the Frosted Flakes?" Suddenly the house shook. "I don't know and I don't care!" she thundered. "I'm not buying that crap anymore! From now on, the sweetest thing you'll find in this house is a graham cracker!" The graham cracker threat was as frequent as it was hollow, but it was an indicator that the house had officially darkened. The situation deteriorated when my brother Mike walked in rubbing his belly, empty cereal bowl in hand, and announced, "My oh my, ain't dem Frosted Flakes like sugah." The standard donnybrook ensued—shouting and brawling and rolling around on the floor as chairs toppled and frightened pets ran for their lives. Mike, who was bigger and a few years older, always had me pinned before I could execute my fantasy move: burying a steak knife in his heart. My father entered the kitchen, separated us, and dispensed with the obligatory "Don't make me knock your fucking heads together," but my mother had had enough. "Dump 'em in the woods," she decreed, her way of requesting that we be dropped off at the Green Hills recreation park, located in the dark thickets off Route 443. (Not as ominous as it sounds: lots of Jews.)

The car ride to the park began unremarkably enough and with a minimum of conversation. I don't recall ever saying much inside my father's car, because it was difficult to remain conscious. Once the Pall Malls were pumping and Bert Kaempfert started oozing from the 8-track player, slipping into a gentle coma was routine. To this day I maintain my dad had stumbled onto a formula that might be of interest to both hypnotists and anesthesiologists. Fortunately, being groggy was usually a blessing when you were in his presence. Merv was a take-no-shit kind of guy. He was tall, built like a block of concrete, and had three basic settings: angry, brooding, and wound-tighter-than-a-gnat's-ass. So it was imperative that you remained perfectly still and quiet in his presence. One errant sneeze would send his shoulders into a startled hunch, followed by an explosive "Jesus Christ! What the fuck's wrong with you?" And lord help the boy who got a case of the giggles, the kind that couldn't be stifled no matter how hard you tried. For this, Merv always offered up the same riddle, delivered in the soothing timbre of a nursery school teacher: "You know what happens to people who laugh too much, don't you?" Heavy beat. "They end up crying." It was a clever little saying and a useful learning tool. It taught me to equate laughter with violence, and permanently wired me to distrust even the slightest flicker of pleasure.

Yet there was an undeniable soft side to my father. When he wasn't being provoked, or avenging a perceived slight, or leaping from the car to kick some motorist's ass, or menacing a stranger for yanking a dog's leash too hard ("How'd you like me to wrap that fucking chain around your neck?"), he could be a real pussycat. This was never more evident than on the ride that day to Green Hills.

Enjoying an open lane and a rare light mood, he pulled out the Bert Kaempfert tape and replaced it with the more life-affirming Al Hirt. The skull-piercing trumpet stabs of "Java" began to ricochet through the car, jolting my brother and me from our hazy sojourn on Queer Street, sponsored by the good folks at R. J. Reynolds Tobacco. The timing of our revival would prove to be unfortunate.

It remains a point of debate as to who saw him first. He was walking along the shoulder of Linglestown Road when our car flew by so fast his gray work shirt billowed and his cap nearly blew off. Mike and I were suddenly wide-eyed and screaming: "Hey, it's Booker! Dad, go back, go back! It's Booker!"

"Who the hell's Booker?"

Booker was the friendly janitor at James Buchanan Elementary School. All the kids loved Booker. He was the only adult in the entire school who didn't treat us like assholes. He did cool things like let us help him get the ladder from the storage closet to get the kickball off the roof or inspect the dead mouse lodged in the motor of the cafeteria milk machine. When we dragged him into the girls' locker room after school one day to find out what the hell was inside that powder blue vending machine on the wall, his answer— "Supplies for the teachers"—was so dull and honest that we promptly lost interest. Man, did we love the guy. The fact that he was colored made him even cooler. We hung on his every word and gesture. And, boy, could he whistle! Booker belonged on television.

"You gotta give him a ride, Dad!" we implored. "He's a nice guy!"

My father didn't hesitate. He made a screechy Jack Webb U-turn and a moment later the big Delta 88 was pulling up alongside Booker.

"Hey there, Booker," my dad called out as the electric window lowered. "Need a lift?"

"Well, if you don't mind, thank you," came the reply.

Mike and I were delirious, cheering from the back of the car as our hero slid into the passenger seat next to my father. This was the kind of thing you dreamed about.

"Where can we take you, Booker?" we shrieked. "We'll take you anywhere! You wanna get ice cream? You wanna go bowling? You wanna come to our house?" My dad shot us a look in the rearview mirror.

Booker rubbed the back of his neck and said, "Well, I was hopin' to get downtown to the hospital to see my sister." Harrisburg Hospital was far in the opposite direction, so I wasn't sure how Merv would respond.

"Don't worry, we'll get you there," my father assured him, clearly satisfied with the boundaries of the mission. He turned up "Java" and we were on our way. It was seamless.

As we negotiated the anemic landscape of Susquehanna Township, Merv talked of his own sister—my aunt Lucy—

who, he said, had also been hospitalized recently with a condition that required her to consume two and a half gallons of water a day:

"I'd visit her a few times a week, Booker, like clockwork. That can be better than all the water in the world. Don't let these doctors bullshit you." Booker nodded.

"How's everything with your sister?" Merv asked. "Nothing serious, I hope."

Booker replied, "Oh, she jus' work in the lunchroom."

My father solemnly knocked on the vinyl dashboard a few times and said, "God bless her. Let's keep it that way."

Mike and I were getting a little annoyed that Merv was hogging Booker. We had a few things to talk about ourselves—urgent topics that came tumbling from our mouths as we gripped the headrests and leaned into the front seat.

"Hey, Booker, remember the time you needed that bucket? And you asked us to get it for you? And we went and got it, and then you gave us some candy from the teachers' lounge?"

Merv disliked rapid, unfocused chatter. Like most things, it made him tense.

"And the time the praying mantis was on the wall in the art room, and Mr. Dunn tried to get it off with a hanger, but it jumped down and you caught it in that mayonnaise jar, but its head fell off—"

"Okay," Merv said, "we understand."

"—and the time Mrs. Weihbrecht asked you to wash her car? And you made that face, and she said, 'Don't make that face at me,' and you said something back to her, and she turned all red and tried to get you fired?"

"Boys—drop it."

"And what about the time Matt Strohecker took a shit in the bathroom sink! And you chased him out with a mop! And he fell and hit his head on the—"

"Shut the fuck up!"

The entire car shuddered as if we'd encountered a wind shear. "The man's off work—let him enjoy his weekend, for Christ's sake!"

He turned to our passenger. "Sorry, Booker."

Booker just chuckled and said, "Aw, them's good boys. Heh-heh. They okay."

He turned around and smiled at us, flashing a gold tooth and pushing his cap back to scratch his forehead.

That was the moment my brother and I realized that the gentleman in the front seat with my father wasn't Booker. Booker didn't have a gold tooth. Nor was he missing a tiny piece of his lower lip. In fact, this man looked nothing like Booker. He seemed nice enough, that's for sure, but again, *not Booker.*

It's difficult to describe the wave of fear that overtook us. Merv's temper could be triggered by anything that caught him off guard or reasonable human error. Things like accidentally dropping your fork at the dinner table, shuffling a deck of cards, or petting the dog too loudly (yes, it's possible). So it was safe to assume that if he discovered Mike and I had put an unfamiliar black man in the car, well, it wouldn't be ideal. Our fate now rested in the hands of the enigmatic pilgrim in the front seat, and we prayed that the words "Why you keep callin' me Booker?" never rolled off his tongue. From this point forward, as far as we were concerned, the guy *was Booker*. He had to be.

The good news was, "Booker" wasn't saying much. Merv continued to do all the talking, choosing topics, I assumed, he felt would be of particular interest to our guest.

"You may not know this, Booker, but I played second-string varsity halfback my sophomore year at William Penn. Then I found basketball. That was my real game. The guys on the other team used to piss in their pants when they'd see me. I got every fucking rebound. You hear me, Booker? I *owned* the backboard."

I could see the back of Booker's head bobbing in polite agreement.

"Yeah, I had those rednecks trained like cocker spaniels. They only had to fuck with me once and, I can assure you, they didn't fuck with me again."

My father swore around everybody. Children, kings, or

clergy, it didn't matter. He exploded into this world untethered from decorum and was incapable of communicating any other way. If you gave a team of speech pathologists five years and fifty million dollars, they'd never be able to get Merv to stop saying "fuck."

"Yeah, I used to swat those fucking hillbillies around like they were horseflies," he continued. "Christ, when we played Steelton, it was a free-for-all. They're not civilized in Steelton. Bunch of drunks. Townies, we called 'em. I fell into the bleachers once and a lady beat me with a metal crutch. Real Okies, you know?"

A small chuckle came from Booker. "She really give it to ya, huh?"

"Ah, fuck her. We were unbeatable. I was out with a sprained ankle for a month and we lost every game. See, I owned the fucking backboard."

We stopped for gas at the Arco station on Sixth Street. While the attendant filled the tank, my father instructed Mike and me to run inside and get a few Cokes.

"You want a Coke, Booker?" he asked.

Booker replied, "Naw, it's that pop that took half my teeth by now. Heh-heh." Merv didn't quite know how to process that information and was further flustered when Mike followed up with "So how many should we get?"

"Just get the goddamn Cokes!" he barked.

My brother and I dragged ourselves from the backseat as Merv let out a frustrated sigh, remarking to Booker, "These fucking kids move like Stepin Fetchit."

The Coke machine was out of order, but that was the least of our concerns. Inside the gas station, Mike and I were finally alone and could discuss our dilemma out loud. We were panicked and irrational, and things swiftly turned heated. Who was responsible for the mock Booker inside our father's Oldsmobile? Mike blamed me, I blamed him, and in a fleeting moment of détente, we both blamed Al Hirt. I suggested we pull Merv aside now and confess, while we were safely parked, rather than risk a car wreck when he figured it out. Mike told me to keep my mouth shut. He wanted to roll the dice. So far, the fake Booker didn't seem to mind being the real Booker.

We debated a bit more and then it turned cheap.

I called him a fuckhead, he punched me in the arm, and I tried to strangle him. Soon we were rolling around the gas station floor in a blur of blue denim and madras. I managed to pry off one of his Keds and launched it into space. It crashed against the metal venetian blinds and filled the small room with an oily cloud of dust that had us both coughing like coal miners. In short order, Mike pinned me under his knees, where all I could do was flail around like an upended turtle. Somehow I kicked over a display rack, and a torrent of road maps rained down on us. I remember having a brief moment to think, *Wow, Delaware,* before I suddenly rose into the sky, as if my spirit was exiting my body. Mike was promptly up there with me.

Merv had us both by the wrists like he was dangling a couple of ratty stuffed animals. A toothless mechanic with the name "Dud" sewn on his coveralls stood there cackling as he wedged a gob of Red Man into his cheek. "I put mine in the shed last Sundee." Merv shot him an annoyed look, the kind he reserved for interlopers and people who owned sheds.

We were swiftly propelled out the door. Mike got a kick in the ass as he walked toward the car. I was in the clear until I laughed, then got one too. "I can't believe you guys came from my balls," Merv grumbled. We heard that one a lot when we did something wrong. It was my dad's version of an Atticus Finch moment, minus the porch swing and gentle wisdom.

Back behind the wheel, Merv turned to Booker as if he had the worst possible news. "Booker," he said somberly, "the Coke machine was out of order. There are no Cokes. I can't tell you how sorry I am." His hand rested on our passenger's shoulder. Booker, who didn't want a Coke in the first place, took it in stride. "Tha's all right," he said. "The world done pretty good with water up to now. Heh-heh." Merv chuckled and agreed. Then Mike and I joined in, laughing a little too hard in an attempt to keep the mood light. "Ha-ha!" I belted out, literally slapping my knee. "Water's still the best drink in the world! Right, Dad? And it's free too! Ha-ha! Water!" Merv's eyes were quickly in the rearview, shooting me an urgent dispatch to cut the shit.

Booker glanced at his watch.

The sky was turning overcast as we journeyed south across Front Street, parallel to the Susquehanna River, leisurely making our way toward the hospital.

"I do two hundred and fifty push-ups every morning," my dad informed Booker as he ignited another cigarette. "My doctor looks at me like I'm a freak. He gave me a stress test and I almost burned the fucking machine out."

Booker's shoulders had fallen into a mild slump—the posture of a man on a bus ride from Bangor to Corpus Christi.

"But I've always maintained my body," Merv went on. "It's my natural instinct. I remember once when I was a kid, I hugged my grandmother so hard I broke three of her ribs. See, I don't know how to regulate my strength. If I hold a canary in my hand, I'll crush it. It's heartbreaking."

"Ol' grandma," a drained Booker murmured, now phoning it in.

"I got in so many fights the social worker came to my mother and told her I was going to wind up either in reform school or the electric chair.

"Almos' had you choppin' rocks."

"I never started a fight in my life, but I took shit from no one. See, everyone was pissed off back then. No one had money. We were all fucking starving."

Merv delicately spat a loose piece of tobacco from his tongue.

"I remember I beat the shit out of this one prick who shot my cat with a BB gun. He said, 'I don't like Jews and I don't like Jew cats.' I told him very sweetly, 'Well, this Jew's about to shove that fucking gun up your ass.' It was a Daisy—I can still picture it."

"Uh-oh. So Daisy got it, huh?" Booker remarked, his attention span justifiably on the wane.

"No, the gun was a Daisy," my father clarified.

"Yeah, ol' Daisy did the jump and run," Booker responded, still on autopilot.

"No, the name of the gun, the outfit that made it, was Daisy."

"Daisy say, 'I'm gonna find me a tree and set there.' Heh-heh."

"Well, again, Daisy wasn't the name of the cat. I'm speaking purely of the BB gun."

I detected a hint of irritability in my father's voice. Mike and I exchanged worried glances, imagining where this might be headed:

Merv: "For the last fucking time, Daisy was not the name of the fucking cat! It was the company that made the gun. Are we clear now, Booker?"

Booker: "Oh, we clear. We certainly clear, 'cept on one thing: Why you keep callin' me Booker, motherfucker?"

Thankfully, such an exchange never took place. Merv continued to display an incredible reserve of patience with our guest, something he would not have afforded me in a similar conversation. It kind of pissed me off. As they went back and forth with their little vaudeville routine (likely known as "The Daisy Bit" on the circuit), I could take no more.

"Jeez, Dad, forget about the gun!" I blurted out. "What was the name of your cat?"

"What the fuck difference does it make?" Merv snapped. "I called him Red. He didn't have a name!"

"If you called him Red, then he *did* have a name."

"Are you being a wiseass? 'Cause I'll put this fucking car in the river right now."

I detected a fatigued sigh from Booker. If he had cracked opened a fortune cookie at that moment, it would've read *Be wary of rides from strangers.*

Roadwork slowed us to a crawl for the next mile or two, and the car grew quiet. My dad had talked himself out, and Booker's head was leaning against the window. In the reflection I could see he was resting his eyes. Every now and then,

Merv would glance over at him like a mother checking on her newborn.

I gazed into the ashen waters of the comatose Susquehanna, and I found myself meditating on my relationship with my father. If only, I thought, it could be more like the one he enjoyed with the stranger in the front seat whom he'd known for less than half an hour. I tried desperately to identify the elusive qualities the man possessed, hoping perhaps I could emulate them, but all I could come up with was:

1. He was pleasant.
2. He was colored.
3. He'd been walking alongside the road.

Clearly there was no cracking it.

The congestion finally let up, and we were flagged into a detour lane. Naturally, Merv saw this as an opportunity to jump on the gas, because only a schmuck would do something like ease back into traffic. The Olds made a head-snapping lurch, startling Booker from his catnap. His eyes shot open and he appeared disoriented and anxious, as if he were stuck in the middle of a bad dream.

"This is where I'm going," he said in a panicked voice.

"I'm getting out right here!" His hand gripped the door handle, and for a moment it looked like he might jump from the moving car. My father gently took hold of his arm.

"We're almost at the hospital, Booker. Hold on, pal," he said calmly.

"It's okay, Booker," I heard myself say, addressing him by his appointed alias. "We're almost there."

Booker collected himself and allowed the cobwebs to clear. He kept looking back and forth between my father and the passing street signs that brought him closer to his destination. Then he seemed to relax.

"Almos' there," he said with a long exhale. "We almos' there."

A sort of calmness came over the car. Even Mike and I started to breathe easy for the first time. You could almost hear the soothing whistle of an aimless wind, as if we were high on a Tibetan mountain.

Then a Chevy El Camino passed us and my father's back noticeably stiffened. "Did you see that, Booker?" he asked. "That thing that looks like it's half car, half truck?" Booker hesitated, perhaps wondering if he could get away without answering.

"Oh yeah, I see him," he finally replied.

"Okay, well, let me tell you something—and please listen

carefully." He took a beat. "Anyone who drives a car like that is an automatic asshole."

For the next several moments, Booker bowed his head, quietly absorbing my father's remark. It was as if he had heard something that required great deliberation.

Then, suddenly, he erupted in laughter.

It wasn't the polite Booker "heh-heh" we'd all come to know, but a body-quaking horselaugh that caused the entire front seat to shake. Booker was probably laughing harder than he'd ever laughed in his life, as though he'd been liberated from something that had troubled him to the point of exhaustion. Mike and I immediately recognized what had taken place. We'd seen it before. This was how people often reacted once they finally "got" our father. Confusion, fear, and even revulsion gave way to acceptance and a sort of enjoyment. Sometimes it took years. Booker got it in under an hour.

Merv was clearly pleased by the response. It fueled his engine.

"I mean, look at that fucking thing," he continued about the El Camino. "What kind of simp walks onto a car lot, looks around, and points to *that*?"

Booker was doubled over, adding his two cents while gasping for air. "Seems like it don't know what it want to be!"

"'Excuse me, Mr. Salesman, do you have something that makes no fucking sense? 'Cause I've got my checkbook out.'"

The front seat was on a roll, so I decided to jump in. "Yeah, Dad, that El Camino guy's a real asshole!" Mike followed up with "I bet you could beat the shit out of him in five seconds!"

"Ah, he's harmless," Merv said. "You don't beat people up for no reason. He's just an idiot."

Atticus had spoken.

We arrived at the hospital parking lot as a light drizzle appeared on the windshield. "And here we are, sir!" my father announced as he wove between two flashing barricades and settled along a section of painted curb marked ABSOLUTELY NO PARKING. He stepped out of the car, walked around to the other side, and opened the door for Booker. Mike and I slid out of the backseat.

This was the clearest look we'd had of our guest all day. It was like standing on the lakeshore and finally seeing the face of a strange fish we'd spent years trying to catch. The man was tall and long-limbed and the waist of his work pants drooped loosely to one hip. He was older and less nimble than the real Booker, and his eyes were fanned with deep lines that retreated into his temples. He smiled at my brother and me and clapped our backs as if we were old comrades who'd once stood side by side in a harrowing battle.

"Y'all look after your pops, hear?" he said.

Then he turned to my dad, shaking off one last chuckle like a chill, and extended his hand. "My man, Jersey Joe. Next time we'll get us one of them truck-cars. Ha!" Merv pulled him into a hug that seemed awkward and unnecessary but fortunately didn't break any ribs.

"Thanks for everything you do for these kids, Booker. They think the world of you. I hope you know that."

I winced. Drop it, already! But Booker just nodded and said, "I ain't worried 'bout these boys. Jus' keep 'em away from ol' Daisy." He let out a hoot. Then he shook my father's hand and walked toward the hospital. He was a few feet away when he stopped and turned around.

"Just call me Sam. Everyone calls me Sam."

"You got it," my dad replied, as if a great honor had been bestowed on him.

As we watched Sam disappear through the revolving door, Merv's enormous paws were on our shoulders, squeezing the tendons so hard that we were hunched over like cripples receiving a savage blessing.

"You guys did a good thing today," he said.

Back on Front Street, Al Hirt had been replaced with the

faint drone of AM radio and a drifting advertisement for Joe, the Motorists' Friend. Mike and I were enjoying a fresh pack of Beemans gum that my dad had pulled from the glove compartment.

As was often the case when he was driving, he was lost in thought. Merv had a habit of looking far away, beyond everything in front of him, contemplating things he would never disclose. I shut my eyes and tried to imagine what they were, to zone in on the mysterious man behind the wheel.

A few seconds later he glanced back and said, "Do you have to chew so fucking loud?"

Playground of the Shrew

Full disclosure: Ever since I was a child, I've loathed all things Disney. There are currently more than three hundred Disney characters, and I hate every one of them. Mickey, Minnie, Tigger, the dwarfs—it's all the same shit to me. "Even J. Worthington Foulfellow from *Pinocchio*?" you gasp. Yup, throw him on the pile. Along with Uncle Walt and his peach-syrup grin, brought on, no doubt, by dreamy reveries of rapidly developing pubescent Mouseketeers.

The plot was hatched hundreds of miles away by my wife's sister, a demanding woman of shrill voice and disagreeable temperament. Diane was a pediatric nurse by trade, and my heart ached for the children under her care. In an act of pure cunning, she called my wife, Lorrie, one evening, and after the usual chitchat about the Anthropologie catalog and their mother's hemophilia, the conversation turned to the kids and spring break.

Diane and her family had been to Disney World several times in the past, and despite her best efforts, she'd been unable to convince us to join them. But now she employed a new slant, a simple brushstroke of propaganda that caught my wife off guard in a weak moment: "Wouldn't it be nice to have the cousins spend time together while they're still young?" It was a clever angle, subtly playing on the "we'll all be dead one day" thing. Personally, I'd rather throw myself in front of the D train than go along on one of these family clambakes, but when my six-year-old daughter, Sadie, begged me, I knew I was fucked. Anything for that kid.

Nothing could've prepared me for the horrors that awaited me in the Sunshine State.

For the record, a person doesn't "visit" Disney World; Disney World sucks you into its digestive tract. Like an anaconda swallowing a wild pig. From the moment you step onto the shuttle at the Orlando airport, they own your stupid ass. Once inside the compound, there will be no escape. All sense of life beyond the park borders fades away. The state of Florida is gone. You are immediately tagged and released into the system. There, you will be scanned, tracked, and relieved of your money via a wristband and a magnetic ID card. Make no mistake, you are here to eat, breathe, sleep, and acquire all that is Disney. Remove your wristband at your own peril. If you thirst, you will not drink. If you wish to meet Princess Jasmine, she will not be receiving.

Diane had us booked at a place called the Wilderness Lodge, located in the Magic Kingdom sector of the compound, abutting the shores of the foreboding Bay Lake. I was grateful to have arrived by bus. I can only assume that a water approach at nighttime, as the fog thickens on the loch, is not unlike Edward Prendick's arrival at the island of Doctor Moreau, with the eyes of queer creatures peering at him through the darkness. Fear not, weary travelers—it's probably just Huey, Dewey, and Louie.

The aesthetics of the hotel were purportedly "inspired by the Great National Park lodges from the turn of the 20th century" and "celebrate the majesty of the unspoiled wilderness." Or, in this case, the architect vomited plastic logs. I detected no natural wood anywhere. If a termite walked in, he'd just say, "Fuck it," and catch the shuttle back to the airport. To be fair, however, the lobby is a giant blow job for aficionados of sacrilegious Native American iconography. So, if you're having night sweats, worried that there might not be a totem pole featuring Disney characters, get some sleep, pal.

Still, I don't think I realized how truly grave my situation was until my first meal on the compound—one of many events Diane would organize without consulting us. A quick heads-up: If you eat on Walt's turf, you eat by his rules. That means the Disney shtick will be rammed down your throat with each tentative bite of Baloo's Maple-Glazed Trout— something I highly suggest avoiding unless you're a fan of fish soaked in pancake syrup.

The Whispering Canyon Cafe is a cavernous shitbox located in the polyurethaned bowels of the Wilderness Lodge. Our server that evening, a stout lass with a wide face seized by rosacea, was decked out in cornball cowgirl attire—a getup she wore as if it had been her destiny since birth. She clomped over to our table and, with a thick Texas drawl worthy of a starring role in the finest production ever put on by a mental institution, loudly announced, "Hi, y'all! I'm Sawdust Sally!" I immediately wanted to kill her.

For the next hour and twenty minutes, this woman would not shut up. Nor would she break character. I have never met a person before or since who was that committed to something. Jihad, by contrast, was a mere hobby for Osama bin Laden. More than once, I politely asked her to "please stop talking that way." But she ignored my request and continued to regale us with tales of "wrasslin' ki-yotes" and "buckarooin'" this and "buckarooin'" that. Sadie sat there frozen with the wary expression she reserves for the homeless guy on Broadway who meows in people's faces. She almost cried when Sally launched into a jaunty tune about branding cattle that had the whole place clapping and singing along. Diane and her kids got so into it, it triggered my acid reflux. Nine days later, when the song finally ended, I kindly asked our lunatic waitress if we'd be eating any time soon, considering we'd ordered the fucking food over an hour ago. She let out a jolly snort and announced to the room, "Yee-ha! We got us a hungry buckaroo here, folks!" Diane and her crew started laughing at me, causing a chain reaction that prompted families from all over the world to laugh at me as well. Humiliated, I decided to pull a one-eighty and join in on the fun. But just as I was about to ask Sally whether it was true that buckaroos were required to soak their cocks in boric acid before trading at the local brothel, the food arrived and I lost interest. I could feel Diane's angry glare as I spat out my first spoonful of Yukon potato leek soup.

Just to clarify, my sister-in-law and I share a deep mutual dislike for each other. Barely a few hours into this escapade and she was already copping an attitude. This was never about "getting the cousins together"; it was about her sick need for control. We engaged in a brief stare-down that ended when a waiter lit a sparkler and her kids went batshit. What the fuck were we doing down here?

The following day we awoke to the pukified orange glow of a Disney dawn. It was time to see the Holy Land.

The Magic Kingdom, the most notorious of Disney World's four theme parks, spans a brain-exploding 107 acres made up of six different "lands," such as Adventureland, Fantasyland, Mickey's Toontown Fair, and if you search hard enough, Geppetto's Glory Hole. Soon, Cinderella Castle loomed before us in all its smaller-and-crummier-looking-in-person splendor. The cousins' eyes lit up instantly. This was their fourth visit to mouse country, and apparently the enchantment comes back like herpes. What really disturbed me was the look on Diane's face. Suddenly possessed of a mad drooling grin, she, too, seemed bewitched by some mystical force that so far had eluded my family and me.

Which brings me to something else I should make clear: In no way am I suggesting that adults who enjoy Disney World with the same passion as their children are vapid dickwits. I'm stating for a fact and putting it into the record that they are vapid dickwits. I saw grown men—*fathers*—wearing Winnie the Pooh T-shirts and having their pictures taken with genies and giant ducks. The expression "Finding your inner child" is just that—an expression. You're not literally supposed to act on it, especially in front of your kids, who see you as their protector.

And speaking of genies and their spray-tanned associates—

yes, you will see Aladdin at Disney World. He walked right by me. So close I could smell his Axe shower gel. I saw Pluto, Donald, those fucking parrots with sombreros, all the creepily muted and bigheaded Disney characters throughout history—everyone except good ol' Uncle Remus from *Song of the South*. I assume the Disney folks considered him a figurative and literal blot on the landscape.

After a few hours of negotiating a host of moldy tent shows and infantile attractions (even by infant standards), I exited the Carousel of Progress with a blinding headache and the sense that I'd lost a third of my intelligence. One thing I did learn, however, is that when kids aren't being enchanted by the Magic Kingdom, they're throwing shitfits. Loud, monkey-screeching, snot-flying shitfits. You can try to get away from them, but rest assured you'll meet again on the plane ride home.

I'd worried about many things over the course of my life, but heatstroke hadn't been one of them. Nobody ever told me that Orlando in March is like the Congo in August. I assumed it would be a little warm, but it was as if something had gone wrong with the sun and gases were expanding exponentially to announce the arrival of the apocalypse. I was getting cranky. Plus, the only place I had even a mild interest in visiting (for reasons I'll keep to myself) was Ariel's Grotto, but apparently the fish-girl was on a five.

It was about this time I realized that Sadie wasn't having fun. No matter how hard her cousins tried to get her into the spirit of something called Mickey's PhilharMagic, she seemed ambivalent, perhaps even confused as to why she wasn't enjoying herself. I think she was also a little put off by the way Diane was screaming at her kids: "Get in that Tiki Room! Don't elbow the gopher! Speak clearly to John Smith from *Pocahontas*!" I knelt down by my daughter and said, "Honey, is there anything special you'd like to—" She cut me off: "Can we go back to the hotel?"

I glared at Diane, who was standing ten yards away, clapping like a baboon at a roving magician who'd just separated two silver rings. I approached and curtly briefed her that we were going back to the hotel to pack our bodies in ice. She looked outraged, as if I were walking out of her son's christening (which I did, by the way). Lorrie stepped in and confirmed that we'd had enough for the day. I detected tension between the sisters, something I considered a personal victory. But just when it seemed the fur might fly, the magician produced a red scarf. Once again, Diane and her tribe were under his spell.

After purchasing three bottles of water that, to my memory, cost nineteen dollars, Lorrie, Sadie, and I began our exodus from the Magic Kingdom.

Somehow, we got lost. The only way back to the Wilderness Lodge was by shuttle or ferry boat. Traveling by boat was out of the question, as I had a premonition of a bearded man in a striped vest playing the banjo. Yet finding the shuttle proved frustrating. No one seemed able—or perhaps willing—to point us in the right direction. *You're leaving? But it's only noon!* I became so desperate I even asked Chip and Dale, but they just shrugged their shoulders like a couple of retards.

Growing panicked, I flagged a security guard and begged him to show us where the buses were located. He gave me a glance and replied, "To the Grand Floridian?" Fun fact: The Grand Floridian is considered by some to be the "Jewish hotel" at Disney World. I guess because it has a spa. I corrected him and said, no, we were staying at the Wilderness Lodge. He scratched the back of his head for a moment, contemplating the unlikelihood of Jews in the wilderness, then gave us some complicated directions he seemed to be making up as he went along. When you're desperate, you'll take anything.

What happened next, I believe to this day, was a plot to prevent me from leaving the Magic Kingdom. Word had gotten out; I was being a "difficult guest"—the Disney World equivalent of what Scientologists call a "suppressive person." As the temperature climbed to roughly 120 degrees, our path to freedom was unexpectedly blocked. We had somehow wandered into the Main Street area as a parade had begun and were quickly consumed by a throng of frenzied zealots who cheered wildly at a procession of Disney characters led by Tinker Bell. Ms. Bell, by the way, was safely ensconced in a glittery cagelike basket, no doubt meant to keep her safe from the grabby hands of daddies and recently paroled uncles. Suddenly, a surge of electricity shot through the crowd and the place went nuts. Mickey had appeared on the parade route. He stood in an open car, solemnly nodding his giant head as he acknowledged his fanatical followers with an occasional white-gloved wave. I will abstain from making a reference to Leni Riefenstahl, but I will say I half expected to hear the sound of windows being shattered at the Grand Floridian.

With the roar of the mob still ringing in my head, we arrived back at the Wilderness Lodge, physically and emotionally drained. Entering the lobby, we were greeted by a guy in a bear suit dancing with a broom. Sadie shrieked, "Oh God, now they're here too?" Later I drifted off into a disturbing sleep, dreaming that I was lying in a battlefield with my stomach ripped open and my guts hanging out. A medic with comical buckteeth was kneeling beside me, delicately removing little pigs with fiddles from my body cavity.

The next two days went by in a blur of dread and fatigue. More heat, more noise, bigger crowds, and the Mexico Pavilion. I felt light-headed much of the time and developed a rash from some off-brand sunscreen I'd purchased from a vendor who, according to the lady behind me, had played the fat kid in *The Bad News Bears*. ("He looks terrible, doesn't he?")

By now, the tension between me and Diane was so thick you could cut it with a pickax, the kind a dwarf might sling over his shoulder before departing for work. The fuse had been lit way back at the Whispering Canyon Cafe, which was connected to the original fuse that had been lit the day we'd first met. Something was going to blow.

There's a phrase the old folks back home like to use when describing one's distaste for an unpleasant task or chore: "I need that like I need a second asshole." So it goes without saying that something called the Tomorrowland Terrace Fireworks Dessert Party would be the granddaddy of redundant assholes. Diane announced—as if it were the greatest news since they started crossbreeding pugs with beagles—that she had made reservations for all of us at the Dessert Party that evening. She was fucking with me, baiting me into battle at that very moment. But I denied her the victory. To her utter confusion, I cheerfully agreed to attend the affair and even said something to the effect of "Boy, I bet the desserts are gonna be dynamite." Ha-ha. No, I would write the final scene in our little playlet, to be performed at a time of my choosing.

To avoid any geographical confusion, the Tomorrowland Terrace is located in the Magic Kingdom, directly down the walkway from the Tomorrowland Noodle Station (to the best of my knowledge, the only Asian restaurant in our galaxy that serves hot dogs). When we finally arrived at the Terrace, it wasn't a vision of the future I found, but essentially a late 1970s high school cafeteria. I kept looking around for Steve Eichhorn so I could tell him to cool it with the quaaludes and not to go to Sue Brenner's party because he was going to drive into someone's living room on the way home.

The much anticipated dessert buffet lay before us, spread out on long steel tables like a Christmas party at the city morgue. And believe me when I tell you, children and adults alike swarmed that shit like crows on a dead groundhog.

It didn't take long before every kid in the Terrace was junked up on sugar and running all over the joint, knocking over chairs, upending café tables, and mowing down toddlers. It was like reliving the Rodney King verdict. You'd think a responsible parent or two might've uttered the magic words "Settle the fuck down," but nah. Why spoil perfection?

All at once, the lights dimmed and you could hear a pin drop. Children settled into their mothers' laps, siblings who'd been fighting just moments before held hands, and all eyes were on Cinderella Castle, now bathed in purple light. Diane and her family soberly gazed upward, as if ready to receive the Eucharist.

Music began. It was one of those drippy, syrupy deathbed

melodies that could come only from the deranged minds at Disney. And then, a honey-bathed voice arrived from the heavens (or, to be more precise, a loudspeaker above the restroom doors).

Star light, star bright, first star I see tonight. I wish I may, I wish I might, have the wish I wish tonight.

A blotch of light now appeared above the castle and shot across the sky. The Kingdom erupted in cheers that could be heard all the way from the Hall of Presidents to the Swiss Family Treehouse.

Tinker Bell!

She was flying at great personal risk along a length of piano wire to the delight of her minions. There was a communal, almost otherworldly sigh from the people standing behind me, and I felt a hot blast of mud pie breath on the back of my neck. Funny thing though: As she flew closer to Tomorrowland Terrace, I noticed that this Tinker Bell didn't quite resemble the pert little thing I'd seen in the parade. No, this Tinker Bell looked like a dude, and a scared one at that. He stiffly waved his magic wand a few times, trying to avoid unnecessary movement. I offhandedly cracked to Lorrie, "Wow, old Tink needs a shave." And with that seemingly benign comment, fireworks exploded above the castle and the walls came a-tumblin' down.

Apparently my voice had been louder than I'd intended,

because there was an audible gasp behind me and a family moved away from us. This did not go unnoticed by Diane. As fireworks blasted and the voice of Jiminy Cricket came over the loudspeaker, sounding like Jim Jones in Guyana, she grabbed me by the arm and hustled me to the edge of the Terrace.

"You're ruining this trip for everyone!" she hissed. Her eyes were ablaze as mouse-shaped rosettes bloomed in her corneas.

"What did I do?" I asked with the face of an altar boy.

"You can't say things like that in front of children! You can't say Tinker Bell is a man! Besides, it's not true!"

With mock indignation, I responded that I really didn't care *what* he was, and neither should she—he's a human being and deserves our support.

"You're an asshole!" she screeched. "I fucking hate you!"

"Well, the skin's off the turkey leg now, ain't it!" I replied in my best hillbilly twang.

"I knew it was a mistake to invite you down here!" she raged. "I will never ask you to do another thing with us as long as I live!"

"I'll believe it when I see it, honey."

The word "honey" produced the desired effect, and she unloaded with a series of insults and expletives, scoring nicely with "burrhead" (God, I hate my hair), but less so with "dumb fuck" (while no intellectual, I'm far from *dumb*).

She still wasn't through, though. It was time to grill me on a litany of past crimes that she'd been stewing about for ages. I was nothing if not an honest defendant.

"Why didn't you come to Riley's play last year?" she snarled.

"I'm not a big fan of the theater," I responded. "Especially when it involves driving five hours to watch a six-year-old pick up a hat."

"He had a line!"

"Forgive me—'I found a hat.'"

"What about Wyatt's sixth-grade graduation?"

"In that case, I purely didn't give a shit."

The pathological narcissist with the Ichabod Crane body and Muppet eyebrows plowed forward.

"Why do you always run out on errands when you visit us?"

"Because I'd rather spend three hours at the Mobile station reading fishing magazines than listen to a blow-by-blow of your latest adventures in electrolysis, which, by the way, ain't working."

It all felt so exhilarating!

A vein emerged on her forehead. Her final query was obviously "the big one." She spoke it slowly and precisely, through clenched teeth. I remember thinking she was either channeling Clint Eastwood or having a stroke.

"Last Christmas," she began, "when I came to New York with my neighbors . . . and I called you from the street—"

I cut her off. "I lied about the broken elevator so you wouldn't come up and use the bathroom."

Her jaw fell and the vein in her forehead did a little dance. I almost tossed it a quarter.

"Barb had interstitial cystitis!" she shrieked.

I don't know who Barb is, and I know even less about interstitial cystitis, but here's the real story: Diane and her pals came into the city to see *Mamma Mia!* and needed a place to park their Lee relaxed fits until the bus carted them back to Pennsyltucky. The bathroom thing was just a ploy to take over my apartment for a few hours.

The memory of the incident got under my skin as I grasped the sheer number of man-hours I'd put in over the years dodging and lying my way out of this woman's demands on my time.

I was through jousting. It was time to burn this bridge to the ground.

I started off slowly and reasonably, admitting that while I was far from perfect, Diane possessed no redeeming qualities whatsoever. Drawing inspiration from the Honorable Minister Louis Farrakhan, I began tossing out words like "wicked," "uncivilized," and at one point, I believe, "enemy of God."

Out of the corner of my eye, I saw a man staring at me with an intense grin, like the guy in *One Flew Over the Cuckoo's Nest* who silently urges McMurphy to strangle the nurse.

I ended my tirade by doing something I hated to do but was necessary to topple the Diane regime once and for all: I ratted out my wife. "And by the way," I said casually, "it was Lorrie who came up with the broken elevator. I wanted to go with bedbugs, but she said that wouldn't be enough to keep you out." Diane looked stunned.

She gazed through me at some invisible spot in the distance. Perhaps, I thought, she was finally reflecting on her selfish need to impose social requirements on my family and me. Or maybe she was consumed with guilt over the number of times she had obnoxiously insinuated herself into my life and the lives of others. Or maybe, just maybe, I was witnessing a spiritual transformation before my very eyes.

But no. She had merely been thinking of another bad name to call me. ("Piece of shit." Yawn.)

And with that, she grabbed her family and stormed out of Tomorrowland and my life. It all happened so quickly. The fireworks weren't even over and a few éclairs were still left on the table.

I turned and found myself looking to the sky. The cricket was singing over the loudspeaker.

If your heart is in your dream, no request is too extreme. . . .

For the very first time, I could hear the words. Was it really true? Had I been wishing to that special star all along?

My family joined me on the terrace. I put my arm around Lorrie and held Sadie's hand. And then, to my astonishment, I felt my eyes moisten. The Disney Magic had entered my body, if only for a brief moment. I could feel it deep inside me, swinging on a little hammock, saying, "Gotcha, bitch!"

I kneeled before the castle and asked Mickey for His forgiveness. I begged Goofy to absolve me of my sins. And I pleaded with Oliver from *Oliver & Company* to have mercy on my soul. A fine mist swirled around me. This time tomorrow I'd be back in New York, living the life I cherished. Marching in my own parade once again.

Like the movie says, "There's no place like home." (Sorry, Walt, that one's not yours.)

Scientology Down Under

The subway station was packed and chaotic, but I managed to spot the sign: FREE STRESS TESTS. As I elbowed my way closer, I could make out a folding table, a stack of *Dianetics* books, and two fresh-scrubbed young men cheerfully trying to make contact with the averted eyes of scowling commuters. In the middle of the table sat what appeared to be a 1970s-era Radio Shack battery tester. In fact, it was the fabled E-Meter—a special device Scientologists use to measure how fucked up your head is (in my layman's understanding). It would have been easy to dismiss or laugh off, but I was in one of those moods—the kind where I realized my brain's done me no favors in life.

The Scientologists received me like a long-lost brother. There was Randy, a superfriendly white guy in a polo shirt and khakis, and Tony, a superfriendly white guy in a polo shirt and khakis who was taller than Randy. They were both trim, well groomed, and energetic. I was fatigued, had a zit in the corner of my eye, and was holding a paper bag with a Bugs Bunny DVD inside. Maybe something good would come of this.

They sat me down on a folding chair, we exchanged pleasantries, and somewhere in the middle of it all, I found myself holding two metal pipes connected to the E-Meter. I was facing Randy. Tony, who appeared to be the more seasoned of the two, stood quietly in the background, observing.

"Adam, I want you to think about something that upsets you," Randy began. "Maybe it's someone you know, someone who's caused you pain. Try to tap into the anger or negative thought patterns you experience during the course of a typical day."

Right off the bat, I felt like a kid in a candy store. The only thing that gets me out of bed in the morning is bitterness, self-loathing, and fantasies of vengeance. Gesturing to the E-Meter, I jokingly said, "Gee, I hope you've got fresh batteries in that thing. You might want to hook it up to a generator." I wanted to keep the mood light to offset my sudden concern that I was going to wind up in a closet with a bowl of oatmeal and holes drilled into my skull.

"*Focus*, Adam," Randy instructed.

I realized this might prove difficult. Between blaring an-
nouncements reminding people to report suspicious packages
and a man washing his feet a few yards away, "focus" was
going to be a tough nut. And then there was the lady dragging the steamer trunk from one end of the station to the
other, shouting, "Roy! Roy! Over here! Roy!" Thankfully that
subsided when she stopped to buy a churro.

"Think about your personal relationships, Adam. *Block
out the noise*. Concentrate on something that invokes deep,
negative feelings."

Again, this should have been like petitioning a dog to eat
a hamburger.

I gripped the pipes like a kamikaze and prepared to dive-
bomb that fortified bunker of animus known as my head. But
I was distracted by a clam-heavy rendition of "In the Mood"
being banged out on a steel drum somewhere in the vicinity
of my left ear.

"Think, Adam!" Randy implored. "Think of anyone
who's ever made you unhappy in life!" I went for the low-
hanging fruit, trying to envision a few of my asshole brothers. But I couldn't muster up the requisite anger.

"Maybe it's a friend who betrayed you. Or an authority
figure from your childhood . . ."

I felt something bounce off the side of my head. It was

a new pair of tube socks with the tag still attached. I had little time to consider the event; the guy with the steel drum was now beating the shit out of "Help Me, Rhonda," which caused my teeth to vibrate. Randy was obliged to raise his voice a few decibels. "A DUPLICITOUS COLLEAGUE! A FORMER LOVER! SOMEONE CONNECTED TO LAW ENFORCEMENT!"

A bony-looking man wearing a Mets cap and a Tropicana orange juice T-shirt appeared to collect the tube socks and wandered off.

The pressure was getting to me. Lord knows I tried, but I couldn't get the needle on the E-Meter to budge. Metaphorically speaking, I felt like those guys you read about who can't "get hard" when they try to perform intercourse. The old-timers called it "whiskey dick," according to my exhaustive research.

Making matters worse, my mind started drifting to all the things in life I was grateful for—my wife and daughter, having a roof over my head, easy access to food and potable water. To my abject horror, I was counting my blessings. Of all the fucked-up timing.

I looked up at the Scientologists apologetically, assuring them I had a vast capacity for rage and negativity and just needed a few more seconds to get my shit together. They had chosen this venue, not me. If their mission was to hawk bootleg copies of the new Ludacris CD, I'd understand, but how did they expect people to self-reflect in a setting that felt like the cutting floor in the Hormel factory?

But there was no turning back. I was committed to getting a stress test, and it was time to close my eyes and seal the deal. Technically, it may have been cheating, but I started thinking about folks like Joseph McCarthy, Pol Pot, and Henry Ford. I even threw in Lansford Hastings, the douche bag who sold the Donner Party on a shortcut to California, but still, I couldn't get my dander up; my mind was a slave to the calypso man and a new guy playing "Big Noise From Winnetka" on a cardboard box.

Meanwhile, Randy, the game apprentice, the bright, eager, puppy-dog life force who epitomized the future of the church, was starting to lose confidence. It was heartbreaking to witness. Tony quickly stepped in and took control of the audit, bringing with him an I'm-not-here-to-fuck-around level of intensity.

"You're fighting it, Adam! You need to block out the environment! You need to *focus*!"

I was sweating.

"Were you ever molested?! Were you ever abused?! Did an adult ever harm you as a child?!"

Just as I managed to dredge up the faint image of a friendly old man who used to live next door to my grandmother, Tony seemed to throw in the towel. In a dramatic Hail Mary play, he took hold of my hand, picked up a copy of *Dianetics*, and forcefully pressed it into my palm. "Adam, you *need this book*!" he bellowed as he knelt before me. But the big moment was interrupted by a gaggle of lively teenagers who scampered by and accidently bumped into the table, knocking the stack of Scientology books to the ground. One of them caught a glimpse of Tony as he flashed a reflexive look of irritation, dismay, and—I'm just postulating here—seething bigotry. The young man—a smidge large for his age—doubled back and slapped the E-Meter off the table. "You want somethin', motherfucker?" he inquired of the Scientologist, who was still holding my hand.

I can't speak for Tony, but I'm fairly certain I've never been called a faggot that many times before in my life. All the variants were offered: "What up, faggots?" "You wanna fuck with me, faggots?" "Y'all gonna fuck each other in the ass, faggots?" He was a fountain of curiosity, this young man. And it suddenly occurred to me: *here* was the perfect candidate for the E-Meter. The stress in his voice was unmistakable. He obviously had deep-rooted anger issues that I assumed harkened back to well before the Civil War. I was about to suggest he take my place at the table, but circumstances prevented it.

After extending numerous (and clearly insincere) invitations to Tony and myself to suck his dick, the kid kicked the E-Meter, which went sailing like a hockey puck and disappeared beneath a shoeshine stand. Then he ran off with his colleagues amid gales of laughter that reverberated through the tiled canyons of the subway station.

From somewhere down on the express track I heard "Roy! Roy! Over here! Roy!"

It was just me and the Scientologists again. Tony, justifiably flustered, silently rose to his feet. He removed the book from my hand and tossed it back on the table. Then he retrieved the E-Meter, which thankfully looked no worse for wear. Randy joined him as they collected stray books scattered about the station floor. No one said much of anything. I helped pick up a few copies, but neither seemed to notice. The boys were down in the dumps, and I was looking for a clean getaway. "Hey, guys," I offered cheerfully, "maybe I'll stop by the church one day and we can try this again in a quieter setting. You're over there in the mid-Forties, right?"

Tony, who was straightening a bent corner on one of the books, gave me a lifeless "Yeah, whatever." He probably sensed I was full of shit.

With the enthusiasm for my presence officially depleted, I slowly crept away. Part of me felt guilty for making things so hard for the Scientologists, yet another part thought, *Fuck these guys. I did the best I could.*

Or did I? At the end of the day, isn't everything my fault? Hasn't it always been that way?

I stopped at the newsstand to buy an Aquafina and a pack of Orbit. I screwed off the cap and—*WHAM!*—just as easy as you please, every prick who's ever distressed, wounded, or fucked me over came flooding back to my head. Some were guilty as charged, while others, perhaps, had been unjustly indicted. I couldn't decide whether to run back to Randy and Tony or to add them to the list. Christ, what the hell was wrong with me?

As I mounted the steps leading to Forty-first Street, I glanced back and saw a lady sitting at the Scientology table.

She was gripping the E-Meter and sobbing.

The Panther

My brief flirtation with the occult began harmlessly, driven
in equal parts by my interest in all things macabre and a
compulsive habit of sending away for stuff. By the age of ten,
I'd outgrown the callow days of rubber chocolates and ex-
ploding cigarette loads and was now searching for something
with a little more gravitas. The ball got rolling when I discovered a witchcraft supply catalog laying around my older
brother Mark's room—just another piece of 1970s head shop
clutter among the *Zap Comix* and crushed boxes of banana
E-Z Widers.

The company, Oracle and Pendulum, was located out west
in a mysterious place called Toluca Lake, which I imag-

ined to be a black, gurgling body of water cloaked in a dark forest lousy with imps and naked hags. At the time, the farthest I'd been from Harrisburg was Ocean City, Maryland, so the rest of the country, I presumed, was untamed and barbaric.

My maiden purchase was a bag of magnetic sand. I wanted to ease into this thing. According to the catalog, magnetic sand would bring its recipient happiness and good fortune. It delivered neither and, quite frankly, was a bit of a mess. In the end, it only managed to cast a spell on my mother's vacuum cleaner. (*"Adam! What is this crap?"*) I was equally disappointed with the ineffectual Mystic Wealth and Riches Spray, which smelled suspiciously like Desenex, and if it's all the same to you, I'd rather skip the embarrassing particulars of Madam Lastlonger's Emotion Lotion, which required a visit to the dermatologist. Nonetheless, I continued paging through the catalog, looking for that one special item that might change my life, or at least distract me for a few seconds.

Despite its provocative title, *The Satanic Bible*, I'm sad to say, is about as foreboding as a jar of mayonnaise. But that's not what I thought when I sent the money order off to Toluca Lake; no, I was purchasing a book brimming with possibility, a virtual instruction manual on how to attain dark powers that would, once and for all, keep my fucking brothers at bay. Unfortunately, any fantasies I had of putting into practice the kind of scenarios so neatly dramatized on shows like *Night Gallery* and Dr. Shock's *Scream-In* were quickly doused. Instead of simple, easy-to-do wizardry, the book's path to evil was overly complicated and would require buying a bunch of stuff like gongs and shit. Who has the money for that? What the book did have going for it, however, was its author, the founder of the Church of Satan himself: Anton Szandor LaVey. First of all, it was the coolest fucking name in the world—something that's still not up for debate. But it was his picture on the back cover that delighted me beyond reason: that ghoulishly shaved head, the sinister-looking watchband, and those evil, all-pervading eyes that seemed to say, "Thanks for buying my book, Adam. If there's ever anything I can do for you . . ." I felt somehow, through telepathy perhaps, that I was now on Mr. LaVey's good side— that is to say, his good *bad* side. I didn't have to read the book for it to be useful; all I had to do was prop it up on my dresser. Those thieving brothers would get the message. It actually seemed to work for a while until one day I noticed it was gone, along with three packs of Juicy Fruit and a roll of dimes I had stashed in my pillowcase.

Christmas vacation came and went and my interest in the occult began to wane, replaced by the notion of raising rats and training them to attack people (my brothers), as I'd recently seen in the movie *Willard*. It was a new year and I felt like I needed a change. But the reality of amassing a bunch of rats that would obey my every command swiftly set in, so I never seriously acted on the idea. All I was looking for was a little control. But for me, a kid living at that time, in that town, in that house, I was as powerless as a bag of magnetic sand.

If *The Satanic Bible* bored me to tears, *Robinson Crusoe* caused me to leak spinal fluid. This was a book of such paralyzing dullness that I cursed destiny for allowing Daniel Defoe to survive the Great Plague and all the other crap he lived through back in sixteen-whatever-the-fuck-it-was. *Robinson Crusoe*, in my opinion, remains the ultimate screw job to any living creature with the ability to read or a mere desire for "something to do." And this is coming straight from a guy who read only a few pages of it.

The real enemy, of course, was not Daniel Defoe, but Mr. Ulsh, my fifth-grade English teacher. With his foul demeanor and slicked-back, tar-colored hair, he was practically a dead ringer for Jerry Lewis, and his every waking moment was the nineteenth hour of the telethon. The classroom was his stage, yet he had nothing but contempt for his audience. Those fatigued eyes seemed perpetually cast out the window, allowing him to admire his yellow Datsun 240Z in the parking lot. It was the car of an asshole, magnified a million times when the asshole happens to be a teacher. Yet for all its horsepower, it was never quite fast enough to outrun the hushed, gossipy voices behind his back, the ones who knew his career as a feeder of young minds had only come about as a way to avoid the draft. He was always dour, and the sole kindness he ever displayed was for Sue Carson, a pretty little hick girl he liked to bounce on his lap while the rest of us sweated over some pointless busywork he churned out to avoid teaching. He affectionately called her Pebbles, I suppose for the rusty ponytail she wore high on her head or the slight tatter to her one and only blouse. Even at age ten I knew his interest in the young Miss Flintstone was, to use a kind, nonlitigious term, "unprofessional." Of all the kids in his class, Ulsh seemed to take a particular disliking toward me. I'm sure my atrocious work habits had something to do with it, but more so, I think he sensed I considered him a stooge. It was a bill inevitably to come due.

The assignment was pure Ulsh: we were to read *Robinson Crusoe* and write a five-page book report over Christmas break. What a sweetheart, this fucking draft dodger, spoiling everyone's vacation while he likely jetted off to the Bahamas with Pebbles. The other kids were justifiably dismayed, but I didn't break a sweat. When it came to schoolwork, I was Mr. Bare Minimum—a superhero who could not be defeated, because I strove for nothing.

I skimmed perhaps half a dozen pages of the book, all out of sequence, but ultimately relied on the handy synopsis on the back cover. From this I fashioned five pages of large handwritten text consisting of double-talk, repetitive horseshit, and roll-the-dice conjecture gleaned from my vague perception that it was a story about a guy stuck on an island. Then I capped it off with a meandering concluding paragraph that ended with the sentence "Robinson Crusoe lived on the island and struggled with his adventures there and then he died there!" The exclamation mark was my way of feigning passion for my work. All I was shooting for was a C-minus and I felt pretty confident. After all, this was Susquehanna Township. We got off every year for the first day of deer season.

The circled red F on the cover page was so fierce that part of it sliced through the paper, and the histrionic all-caps SEE ME!!, underlined three times, was, quite honestly, a bit of a surprise. My misstep had been as simple as it was fatal: apparently Robinson Crusoe did not die on the island—or anywhere else for that matter. He remained alive and well to the very last period on the last page. In my defense, this was not something I could've possibly known, having read only one-fiftieth of the book.

Pursuant to Mr. Ulsh's instructions, I SAW HIM!! after class. He made me sweat it out for a few minutes before bucking Pebbles off his lap and sending her to lunch. Then he closed the door, which I found a little over-the-top. "So tell me," he said, perching himself regally on the corner of his lopsided tank desk, "how did Robinson Crusoe die on the island?" I kept my head down and stared at his shoes. They swung lazily, like some rich Southern belle on a porch swing who thinks the whole world wants to fuck her. He repeated the question, this time adding a dash of unnecessary ball-busting: "How did Robinson Crusoe die on the island? Did he get hit on the head by a coconut? Did he get run over by a bus? Enlighten me." I just shrugged, refusing to look up. Several more queries were machine-gunned in my direction, ending with the supremely patronizing "What day of the week did Robinson Crusoe name Friday after?" Fearful it was a trick question, I didn't respond. It was news to me there even *was* a character with that name. Thank God, he didn't know what I was thinking—that Friday was most likely a baby gorilla. Through toying with his prey, it was time to eat. His eyes seemed to milk over and his acne scars reddened as he imposed his sentence: I was to read the entire (!) book, cover to cover, and write a fifteen-page report, due by the end of the month. *Fifteen pages!* Was he mad? There were only so many words in the English language. I suddenly felt dopey, and the bones in my feet melted. I had to sit down.

"And listen carefully," he pronounced, "if I read one word of bullshit, one *syllable*, your ass is grass." It was an expression I didn't understand then and don't understand now, but I was sufficiently terrified. The tears I was trying to avoid pulled into the station. Finally, I had pleased my teacher.

Doing the required work was never a consideration; put a gun to my head and I freeze like a rabbit. That's one thing those teachers never got over the years—I can't be won over with sanctions and pleas for improvement. Still, I was in a bad spot with this Ulsh business. I staggered home that afternoon, anxiety surging, and more than once contemplated stepping into traffic. That familiar little snowball in my brain had begun its steady roll downhill.

Then, two fortuitous incidents happened within a few days of each other. *The Satanic Bible* mysteriously reappeared in my bedroom—a little grungier and reeking of pot, but Mr. LaVey's villainous face still looked like a million bucks. I never knew which brother took it, or why it was returned, but it didn't matter. I had my man back. Later that week, an unassuming envelope arrived in the mail. The rubber-stamped return address identified the sender simply as M.M.E. and included a post-office box number from the curious town of Hercules, California. Inside, I found a single mimeographed sheet of paper that contained a list of "Hex and Spell Aids." There were no illustrations, no aerosol get-rich sprays, just a tidy menu of voodoo-related merchandise printed in small typeface. The no-frills nature of it screamed integrity; it felt clandestine, unlike the splashier Oracle and Pendulum catalog with its Spencer Gifts pomp and ballyhoo. Having yet to know about such worldly concepts as getting on a mailing list,

I read a great deal into how the envelope magically found its way to my doorstep. And what was M.M.E.? An anagram? Had there only been a Y, I could've rearranged it to spell MEMY, but what would that have gotten me? My mind was racing. Then it hit me like a two-ton crystal ball to the crotch—E is the *fourth letter* in the *last name* of *Anton Szandor LaVey*! Did that rascal have something to do with this? Not only that, but I received the F on my book report on a Tuesday, the fourth day of the week (assuming you start the week on a Saturday), and the number four is only *four numbers* away from eight, my lucky number. It was all adding up—the cryptic return of *The Satanic Bible*, the hex list from Hercules, and the dozen or so other illogical thoughts bouncing around my head. Help had arrived.

I doubt I was the first kid to consider penetrating his teacher's subconscious until he's overcome with fear and confusion and develops a lockjaw-like condition that reduces his speech to the squeals of a dolphin, but give me credit, at least I moved on the idea. According to the description, the "100% genuine African Black Panther Eye" would bring about the above-described conditions to your enemy if you recited a simple incantation and placed the eye among his possessions for a period of forty-eight hours (*another four!*). I quickly recalled the fifth declaration of the Nine Satanic Statements found in *The Satanic Bible*: "Satan represents vengeance instead of turning the other cheek." What more did I need? Ulsh was fucked as far as I was concerned. He'd brought this on himself, and I would execute the hex not only for me but also for every human being whose life had been adversely affected by this piece of shit—from the countless students and a duped Pebbles to the fallen heroes in Southeast Asia who might have been pulled from harm's way had there only been an extra pair of arms to save them.

The eye was fifteen dollars, not a small amount of money, but I could only imagine the expense and sweat equity that went into prying it out of the panther's face and shipping it from Africa to Hercules. I had about forty bucks stashed inside a globe I'd dissembled and modified for storage purposes, one of several makeshift hiding places I was forced to devise due to the endless crime wave in the upstairs hallway. This could very well be the most important purchase of my life.

And so, I waited for a parcel to arrive from the Golden State. As I lay in bed at night, I tried to imagine its journey east. Had it made it to North Dakota yet? Utah? The Panhandle? Like book reports, geography wasn't exactly my thing. And what would the package look like? I envisioned a zombie-eyed mailman requesting my mother's signature for a small wooden box fastened shut with frayed twine and a rusty hook lock. Curiosity getting the best of her, she'd open it, removing handfuls of straw before discovering a little glass vial containing a strange object floating in black liquid. Her eye would meet the panther's. She'd scream and pass out. The vile would shatter, the eye sliding across the kitchen floor. I could see the dog running in and giving the eye an inquisitive sniff before eating it. Soon old Sarge would be acting out of sorts, leaping in the air and trilling like a porpoise. One of my brothers, speculating that our beloved pet might be worth something, would sell him to a carnival, where he'd be abused and beaten like Buck in *The Call of the Wild*, a book I actually read and liked quite a bit before it was stolen from my room. Those fucking brothers. They were next on my to-do list.

I was starting to feel less frightened of Mr. Ulsh, despite an uptick in his menacing taunts. In class I'd sit still and quietly, a cobra in the body of a kid, focusing my gaze at his desk drawers.

Place the panther eye among the victim's possessions for forty-eight hours.

Ah, what a perfect little hidey-hole for a perfect little gift— a special apple for the teacher, nesting in silence among his other . . . *possessions.* I'd clap a hand over my mouth to smother a stray giggle. One afternoon, as I was exiting class, he jabbed at the last day on the calendar and remarked in that tone of his, "We're getting close, wonder boy. Is it coming?"

I nodded meekly, but inside my head, I replied, "Oh, it's coming, Flipper, it's coming . . ."

It was a clear, unseasonably warm Saturday in January, one of those days when everyone comments that it feels like spring and I stay locked in my room with the shades down. I was lying in bed, playing with a little plastic Radio Shack slot machine I'd gotten for Christmas. It ran on two double A batteries and was about the size of a deck of cards. You pushed a button to make the reels spin until they exhausted themselves and gave out. Sometimes three cherries lined up unevenly, which was considered a "win." Pathetically simple and unsophisticated, it felt like a kindred spirit. It required no skill, paid out nothing, and provided no sense of accomplishment. I played it for hours. Suddenly I heard something skid under my door. I glanced over and saw a small padded Jiffy envelope with a tiny bulge in the middle. The slot machine stopped spinning: three panther eyes.

"More crap?" my mother called out from the other side of the door. "What now?"

"Nothing!" I yelled as I jumped up to retrieve the package. "Just something for school!"

"Whatever it is, don't make a mess!"

I heard her walk off.

Don't make a mess. Oh, sweet, adorable Joyce. If only you knew.

The Jiffy envelope was a bit lacking in presentation, but I assumed it was meant to throw off nosy postal inspectors who confiscated the organs of wild animals transported for the express purpose of devil-related shit. My hands were tingling as I yanked the pull tab, opening an ugly gash in the package, which sent a cloud of gray fibrous dust into the air. The intensity of the moment ebbed slightly when I realized my acquisition was wrapped in the Sunday comics section of the *Sacramento Bee* (featuring a predictably lame *Beetle Bailey* strip). I tore it away, uncovering a plastic sandwich bag that contained a balled-up Scott paper towel with a tulip pattern. I had to give it to M.M.E.—they really knew how to throw off those fucking postal inspectors. Extracting the tulip ball, I watched in amazement as it came to life and bloomed in my hand, revealing the star of the show: an almond-shaped dried-out white thing that looked like a piece of chalk. With a monkey's curiosity, I tapped it gently with my fingernail and it promptly broke in half. Even with a 63 average in science, I was fairly certain it wasn't a panther's eye. Inside the sandwich bag, I noticed a little strip of paper, the kind you find in a fortune cookie. It read: *For best results, anoint charm with Conquering Glory Oil, available separately.*

The urgent communiqué I swiftly sent off to Hercules went something like this:

Dear M.M.E.:

I just got this panther eye I ordered from you and I am very PISSED. The eye came broken and does not look like a REAL "panther eye" and you might have sent me something else by mistake because I did not want a CHARM! Please send me a real panther eye by airmail RIGHT AWAY. I need it very quickly which is why I ordered it in the first place! This looks like a piece of chalk and I did not break it, it broke by itself!! Please send me the real panther eye as soon as you read my letter and I don't know what Conquering Glory Oil is because you didn't say I needed it anyway, so send the Conquering Glory Oil too which would be the right thing because I need that and it's the mistake YOU made and I didn't!!!

Adam Resnick

P.S. Please send right away by AIRMAIL after you read this letter!!!

P.S.S. (and I could write a letter to Anton LaVey and tell him if I don't get it!)

By now Ulsh's campaign of harassment was escalating to unprecedented heights. I could barely take three steps from my desk without hearing, "How's the masterpiece coming along, Edison?" or "Counting the seconds, Goldilocks." All the mind-fucking was taking a toll. The end of the month was closing in and there was nothing from Hercules. Never once, though, did I consider even attempting the assignment. It was a fool's errand, and by this point, I was on the verge of an emotional swan dive. I was losing sleep, and during the day I felt weak and disoriented. My jaw ached when I chewed food, and I developed a tic, constantly opening and closing my mouth to test it. Once, I noticed Pebbles watching me from across the cafeteria with a look of disgust. He'd obviously told her everything, making me out to be more horrible than I actually was. Yeah, they all knew by now; everyone was waiting to witness my spectacular downfall. I was convinced Ulsh was hatching a plot to have me flunk fifth grade, preventing me from going to middle school. I'd be remade into one of those droopy-lipped farm kids who were always held back—"special helpers" the teachers called them in a lazy attempt to fan away the retard fumes. Oh, God, what if I became a special helper? What could I expect from my brothers then?

It was a plain white envelope, not a Jiffy mailer, waiting for me on the kitchen counter when I got home from school. The postmark was from Oxnard, California. I ran it upstairs and closed my door. Half-crazed, I tore it open with my teeth and watched a small piece of paper flutter to the bed—it was a credit slip for fifteen dollars. There was no explanations, no "Sorry for the inconvenience," no "Yeah, that last eye was bad, we'll send you a fresh one when they're back in stock"—nothing. But here's where I give my nervous system big props for not losing its shit: the credit slip was redeemable at—figure this out—Oracle and Pendulum. Not only did I not purchase the eye from Oracle and Pendulum, but O&P was located in *Toluca Lake*, not Oxnard, and Oxnard was not Hercules—the home of M.M.E.! I noticed something else inside the envelope and shook it out: a little sticker of a cow in a straw hat with the words "Knott's Berry Farm" on the brim. This marked the beginning of my lifelong hatred for California.

I never stood a chance against the age-old forces of nature set upon earth to crush the wills of ten-year-old boys. The world was ruled by the Mr. Ulshes, and his résumé had been preapproved: adult, teacher, draft dodger; a man who drove a flashy sports car while other people were starving, who bounced cute little girls on his lap while ignoring the plain ones; a vulgar human being who pissed all over the birthday of God's only son by callously assigning a gratuitous book report. The devil and his angels had been in Ulsh's corner all along, enabling him to enter my head like a flotilla of squirming microbes that were slowly turning my brain into vinegar.

And I was probably on LaVey's shit list, too, because I didn't read his book either.

But every now and then, as the walls close in and the ground beneath you slips away, the whirling reels of the neurosis slot machine line up just so, and—click!—*clarity.* There existed in this world a power more frightening than black magic and more volatile than a boxcar hauling nitroglycerin. If handled correctly, this force could be used to resolve seemingly unresolvable matters. But to conjure it, one must tread carefully.

If the name Merv Resnick brings to mind the image of a little Jewish man hunched over a sewing machine in a dress factory, you've got the wrong kike. Picture a multi-vortex tornado sucking on a Pall Mall and you're getting warmer. Created within a swirl of hissing steam that rolled through the streets of a Bronx slum, he emerged tall and muscular and more handsome than any movie star. Like the rest of the refuse, he grew up pissed-off and hungry, gnawing on stolen potatoes charred over newspaper fires. He trusted no one. By the time he was twelve, he'd been in more fights than Joe Louis—using his sledgehammer left to shut the mouths of "those fucking Irish" who'd been genetically programmed to be the most petulant of all immigrants. (That is, if you don't count the Germans.) By the age of fourteen, he'd been stabbed, clubbed, and shot at. But they couldn't kill him. Patient and methodical, he took care of them all, one by one, sometimes waiting for months to serve a brick to an enemy's head. And the shirts—all those bloody shirts the mothers brought to his tenement doorstep: "Look what your boy did to my son! That animal!" they'd screech in excited brogues. That he never initiated trouble was overlooked, and his unyielding sense of justice brought no admiration. Two eyes, a concussion, and a handful of teeth for an eye. There would be no lenience for verbal misdemeanors. Ask Keiser the druggist, who was met with a length of pipe after Merv overheard him mimic his mother's Russian accent. Or the street sweeper who made an ill-advised remark about his grandfather's beard. "Those fucking people ruined me," he once said in a reflective moment. "They took a nice guy and ruined him."

My father was like a rottweiler who protected his family unconditionally, but if you touched that weird spot on his hind leg that bugged him for some reason, you might get your face torn off. You lived in constant fear of him yet never doubted the brutal love he had for you. He wasn't someone you went to for advice, wisdom, or relevant quotes from philosophers. You went to him when you had a problem that could not be solved by any other means, and just prayed he ruled in your favor.

One never approached Merv before he'd eaten; you didn't

walk past him, you didn't say "hi," you just made yourself scarce. My mother would put the food down and run. He ate alone. If he'd found some measure of peace after his meal, you knew it by the way the cigarette smoke hung in the air and how he absentmindedly fingered the snake ring coiled around his pinky. I entered the kitchen in silence, cautiously taking a seat at the table; if I accidently made the chair creak, his blood pressure would surge and I'd be harshly ejected from the room. I quietly stared out the window. It was already dark outside. The safest way to engage in a conversation with my father was to let him come to you. When Merv relaxed, and his intensity level reduced to the vicinity of neutral, something like a low gravelly hum would emanate from deep in his throat. It's impossible to imitate and difficult to describe—as unknowable as the rebel yell of the Confederate soldiers, which exists only in the sketchy descriptions of historians. As I gazed out into the gloom, I finally heard that familiar esophageal vibration. I glanced over. He'd been watching me.

"What's the matter?" he asked.

"I'm having trouble in school," I replied unsteadily.

"Another kid? Why don't you rap him in the fucking mouth?"

"No," I said. "A teacher."

The humming stopped and he crushed out his cigarette.

Our chairs creaked in unison and I let go. I admitted to doing a bad job on a book report, but the teacher wasn't being fair. "He doesn't *like* me," I said. "He makes fun of me; he told me my ass was grass." The kitchen light flickered as if there'd been a power surge. "I just want him to stop being *mean* to me." Merv broke off a piece of sugar cookie for the dog.

"What time does he get there in the morning?"

There was no talk as my father drove me to school the next day. Sinatra was singing "Street of Dreams" on the 8-track, but all I could hear was the hum. Low, steady, present. He was relaxed to the point of almost falling asleep. My dad took care of his own problems. He didn't need Jilly and a crew of goombahs to do it for him.

It was full-strength Merv Resnick I trailed down the hallway of James Buchanan Elementary: the cigarette, the suit, the snake ring. Fuck, just the way he *moved*. It was the first time he'd ever set foot in the school, but by the way he walked, you would have thought he'd built the place with his bare hands. Kids, teachers, and custodians stopped in their tracks and gaped. *My God, who is that?* I'd seen the reaction countless times before, whenever my father entered the space of mortals.

"Where's the room?" he asked with as much emotion as it takes to order a cup of coffee. We approached the door.

There were no kids inside; it was still early. I managed a brief glimpse of Ulsh straightening his desk. "Wait out here," Merv said to me. Then he walked in and closed the door behind him.

All I could see were two shadows behind the frosted glass. There was no movement. I vaguely made out the muffled voice of my father. It was calm. Moments later, the door swung back open and he exited. His cigarette had barely burned down. He patted me on the head, and said, "Okay. Go to school." I stood there and watched him walk off down the hallway, tail swaying, belly full.

I entered the classroom and found Mr. Ulsh standing by the window, gazing at the mountains. He appeared to be trying to comprehend something, something he'd be struggling to sort out for the rest of his life. Maybe his head was at last filled with the sound of ground fire and the suffering of all of those people he let die. He looked shrunken, this man who hated my guts. He slowly turned around and jumped back, as if he'd seen an apparition. Then a wide silly smile came to his face.

"Adam! My man!"

We were suddenly pals. It had all been a big misunderstanding. A lack of communication. And he felt awful about it. "Just clean up the ending a little bit!" he said merrily. "You worry too much!"

So that's what I did: read a few relevant passages, changed a sentence or two, and at long last, Robinson Crusoe was saved. Remarkably, I received a B-minus for my efforts. That, and the enduring respect of my teacher.

The credit slip from Oxnard would remain unredeemed. We'd both been tortured enough.

Substandard Risk

They took me from my mama, an' made a wrecked man out of me
Yeah, they took me from my mama, they made an awful mess of me
Clouds high above me cryin', but these chains they laugh at me
—PRISON WORK SONG (UNDATED)

From the very first bell of first grade, I considered school nothing more than a hard dozen without the possibility of parole. For twelve long years, my only dream was to be a free man of legal age. And on the day of my release, I walked out of that pigeon mill with my head held high. The worst of life was behind me. I had no plans to attend college or find a job. I had no thoughts about my future. My work was done.

That same evening my father told me I'd be going into the insurance business.

The headline was delivered as I was lying on the floor,

eating a bowl of Sugar Smacks and watching cartoons. Apparently no one got the memo I was retired. Soon I found myself pounding my fist on the rug and making lofty declarations about being an adult now and how my parents no longer owned me. I was rebutted with trifles about being "a goddamn bum" and possessing a GPA so low I "couldn't get hired as a fucking circus dog." My father had a knack for simplifying things with confusing statements.

Merv had been an insurance man for most of his adult life, and a few of my brothers had followed him into the business. We Resnick boys were a dim lot, to put it politely, but if there's one thing we knew like the back of our hands, it was our limitations. And for guys like us, a career in sales is the little mockingbird that calls your name on your eighteenth birthday.

I bought myself some time by enrolling at HACC (Harrisburg Area Community College, for all you purists), but kept my course load fairly light. Three classes seemed like plenty, and I was acutely aware of not wanting to burn myself out. This little detour into academia quickly ended, however, when my grades arrived and my parents saw that I was flunking Basic Stagecraft as well as the Automobile in American Literature. One week later, I found myself in a pair of Florsheim Imperials, pulling up to a squat celery-colored building in Lititz, Pennsylvania.

Located in Lancaster County, Lititz is generally considered a dull town even by its comatose neighbors in Ephrata. Nonetheless, it could proudly call itself home to Dirschberger & Associates, the mid-state agency of the Keystone Valley Life Insurance Company. As I stood there, taking in this venerable landmark, I contemplated severing my carotid artery by shoving my head through the window of the adjoining wig shop.

Bob Dirschberger was an old friend of my father's, even though Merv often referred to him as "a first-class putz." I don't know how or why Bob was chosen to be my mentor in "the business," but I suspect my dad figured he was the only guy dumb enough to take me on. Bob greeted me in his office with a laughing grin and a slap on the shoulder. "You ready to rob a few trains, Sundance?"

He was a gregarious and somewhat dashing man, with salt-and-pepper hair and a matching mustache that looked like they came with his suit. The toothy smile, which rarely faded, gave him a passing resemblance to the great character actor Warren Oates. Settling in behind his desk, he pulled out a bottle of Seagram's Five Star and a couple of glasses. I declined because I didn't drink, plus it was eight-thirty in the morning. Bob looked a little disheartened, but then perked up, asking hopefully, "But I bet you like pussy, right?" I assured him I did, and this made him laugh uproariously for a little too long before downing his drink. Then he got very somber and told me his ex-wife was a confused woman and when it was all said and done he felt nothing but pity for her. "You know, they start in with those diet pills and suddenly they're seeing broads in your glove compartment . . ." He took a moment for himself, and then had me by the arm, leading me into the morning meeting. "Let me introduce you to these clowns!"

We entered a small conference room, where Bob introduced me to the other agents as "the kid who's gonna put a flame under all your asses." This failed to cause much of a stir, but I shook a few hands, unsuccessfully avoiding one guy who had orange fingers from eating gas station cheese crackers, and getting a blast of Jovan Musk from another wearing Speedy Gonzales cufflinks. Any pangs of intimidation I may have had quickly faded.

The meeting that day was a short one. Bob kicked things off with a joke about a man who, for reasons that remain unclear, had a wooden penis. The narrative contained such touchstones as a disagreeable prostitute, withheld information, and the jaunty punch line "So long, splinter lips!" After the laughter died down, Bob switched on the overhead projector, the bulb blew out, and he proclaimed, "Fuck it, go to work, you schlubs." As we exited the conference room, he patted my shoulder and said, "Well, my friend, you're off to the races."

Even the great Secretariat began his journey to the Triple Crown with those first wobbly steps as a foal, and I was no different. In order to become a licensed agent, I would have to pass the state insurance exam. Naturally this concerned me, as the absorption of knowledge was never my strength. And the conditions I was forced to study under were less than ideal. Because of water damage in the only spare office, I was given a desk in the common area next to the reception-ist, Helen. Helen was a balding sixty-year-old part-time bar-tender at the VFW who also taught piano on weekends. Most of her days at the agency were spent doodling rabbits on WHILE YOU WERE OUT pads while humming such middle C chestnuts as "Hot Cross Buns" and "Au Clair de la Lune." What I lost in concentration I gained in fantasies of drown-ing her in the toilet.

Not that I could even begin to crack what I was supposed to be learning. This was a bleak piece of work, this insurance manual. Talk about an Aspergian jizz-fest of dry terminology and monotonous concepts. Sometimes I'd have to glance at the state seal on the cover just for entertainment. In what cockeyed reality could anyone think I was qualified to be an insurance salesman? I was a cranky teenage layabout who bought fireworks from the mop guy at Arby's. Was I really the best choice to sit a man down, discuss his mortality, and monkey with his finances?

By late afternoon on most days, the agents would stumble back to the office looking good and beat-up. It was always the same routine: Shane Simons would declare that this was not the business he started out in, Buddy Fowler would crow about some negligible victory ("I got a very good nibble from a fellow who works nights at the quarry"), and Pete Arbaghast would storm Bob's office to bitch about some fiasco that may or may not have been Bob's fault (but usually was).

For me, it was goof-off time when the agents returned. I'd put down the insurance book, stretch, and wander around the office. I quickly discovered that striking up a bullshit conversation with an insurance agent is one of life's easier tasks. For the most part, I gravitated toward Shane because we shared an interest in photography. Shane was a sullen man, but he could get quite animated when talking about filters and f-stops. One day, he brought in his portfolio, and I was genuinely impressed by the sheer number of angles in which he was able to photograph a gutted deer.

After failing the insurance exam three times in a row, I began to detect a pattern, but Bob cheered me on: "Dull knives still cut, Adam. Keep hacking away." Sure enough, the fourth time was the charm. I'll never forget the sight of my mother running from the mailbox to the house, screaming, "He passed it! He passed it!" before tripping and banging her knee on the porch step. She was limping and out of breath by the time she handed me the letter, repeating, "He passed it," still using the third person. I won't deny feeling a sense of accomplishment when I realized I was now licensed to sell life insurance in the state of Pennsylvania. Then it hit me: I was now licensed to sell life insurance in the state of Pennsylvania. The day I swore would never come had arrived: I was a fucking insurance salesman. A thought briefly entered my mind that was so horrible and disturbing it made me feel dizzy: *Should I have tried a little harder in school?*

The one good thing about passing the exam was telling Bob, who was so thrilled that he threw me a little celebration party that evening at the Holiday Inn in Harrisburg. It was just the two of us at the bar, Bob belting down Crown Royals while I feasted on birch beer and Spanish peanuts. He asked me if I was sure I didn't want a drink, and I told him no, I was pregnant. He let that one digest for several seconds before convulsing with laughter. "You know something, Adam? I like you! You're a wise guy!"

Bob put his arm around me and gave me the good news: I was now officially set for life. "In this business, *we* choose what we make," he said loudly. "The sky's the limit. Not like these other slobs who snake drains for a living and beg their wives for a piece of snatch every night." Coincidentally, Bob had failed to sell a policy to a plumber earlier that week. "What do you want to make this year, Adam? Fifty grand? A hundred grand?" Those were outrageously high numbers. Not wanting to sound arrogant, I split the difference and went with seventy-five. "Bullshit!" he thundered. "You're gonna make a hundred grand this year or I'll take a piss all over this bar!" There were people around us, and I gently tried to shush him, but he waved me off, saying, "Hey, Adam, I love you, but I'm not gonna put on a top hat for these animals."

Essentially, though, Bob was what you'd call a "happy drunk." One minute he'd be yapping it up with a man who distributed flange bolts, and the next, shaking his ass on the dance floor with a plump, giggly state worker. The only crimp in the evening was a heated exchange between Bob and the bartender over the tab: "I'd have to be a goddamn sperm whale to drink all this!" It ended agreeably, though, with Bob making nice and hugging him, repeating over and over, "You're a good lad." After we left the hotel, he proudly held up his trophies for the evening: a business card from the flange bolt guy and a scrap of napkin with his dance partner's phone number. "So there you have it, my friend. I'll sell one and bang the other. Can a plumber do that?"

I bid my boss goodnight and watched his Monte Carlo flatten several traffic cones as it fishtailed down Second Street. It was at that moment I formulated my strategy: If the numbers Bob was throwing out were truly possible, all I had to do was work hard for three years and then parachute out with roughly a quarter of a million dollars. That kind of dough buys freedom, which was all I was after. And a Jeep.

Buddy Fowler invited me into his office the next day. A genteel man with the fat, hairless face of a baby, Buddy played French horn in the Leacock Drum and Bugle Corps. Everyone in the agency conspicuously avoided him for fear of hearing the dreaded words "Come on out this Sunday." But it wasn't drill formations Buddy had on his mind this particular morning.

"Adam and Eve!" He chuckled pleasantly as I entered. I chuckled back as if I'd never heard that one before. "Adam," he said, "now that you're a fully licensed agent—and may I offer you a hundred-and-one salutes—I have a very unique business opportunity for you. Normally I would partner with a more seasoned man for a job like this, but I've always had a soft spot for the novice." I observed a small blob of Pepto-Bismol on the carpet next to his desk.

Buddy continued, lowering his voice a bit: "I'd like you to

pick up a check from a gentleman out by Shippensburg named Russ Ziegler. Owns a little auto parts store. He will not be happy to see you, which I apologize for in advance. I need you to tell him the following: Mr. Fowler is no longer with the company. Do you understand, Adam? Advise him that I was diagnosed with pancreatic cancer, and as far as you know, I'm convalescing with an uncle in Birmingham. It's really that simple. If you get the check, and I'm certain you will, there's a fifty-dollar bill on the clothesline for you."

Wow, I thought, *this insurance thing is a breeze.*

The ride to Ziegler's Auto Supply was long and dreamy. The AC in my car had been dead since the day I bought it from Chet Dunlap's brother, but recently antifreeze had been misting through the air vents, which I wisely sealed with duct tape. While my face no longer became glazed with ethylene, the interior still got a little fumy, even with the windows open. *Man, fifty bucks,* I kept thinking as I shook off sleep. *At this rate, I might hit my goal of two hundred and fifty grand earlier than I projected.*

I don't remember how many words I got out before Russ Ziegler started yelling and spraying spit all over me. "You tell Bud Fowler to go fuck himself!" I backed up a bit, knocking over a cardboard cutout of Cale Yarborough holding a spark plug. "I made some calls and I know what he's up to.

My brother-in-law told me I lost three grand on that last policy!"

I had no idea what he was talking about. Buddy had been short on details.

"Well, uh," I stammered, "I'm sure Mr. Fowler, who doesn't work for the company anymore because he lives with his uncle and has cancer, had reasons for telling you stuff that was trying to help you and—"

He cut me off. "He thinks he can sell and resell me a policy every five years? You tell that lying son of a bitch I'll shove that fucking horn down his throat!" Mr. Ziegler's Battle of Inchon crew cut was now turning pink at the scalp, and he instructed me to get the hell out of his store before he broke me over his leg like a Popsicle. I remember thinking: *Wouldn't that be a little awkward, if not messy?*

As I patched out of the parking lot, I made a mental note to come back in a few years when I was more muscular and kick his old-man ass all the way from the fan belts to the wiper blades.

Back at the agency, Buddy sighed and thanked me for my efforts. "Why don't people want to help themselves, Adam?" he asked sadly. "It's life's ultimate mystery." He gave me five dollars for gas and slunk back to his office. Later, Bob somehow got wind of the incident and I heard him lecturing Buddy in the hallway: "That kid's not your goddamn janitor. Next time clean up your own shit." On his way out that night, Buddy handed me another five bucks and a flyer for an upcoming parade in Mount Gretna.

My phone rang early the next day. It was Bob, informing me that it was officially time to get my hands dirty and "start selling this crap." He'd cleared his schedule for the day and was going to train me personally. Still feeling bad about the Buddy thing, he advised me to be wary of agents asking for favors. "Those other guys tend to overcomplicate their jobs sometimes. Stick with me and I'll keep you out of Alcatraz."

I met Bob at Colonial Park Plaza, where his plan was to teach me, as he termed it, "the miraculous little foxhunt known as 'cold calling.'" He stood there like an Indian wise man, making assessments in his head while silently looking up and down the mall. Finally, he declared: "Yeah, this'll be a fucking log ride." Then he reminded me of two things before we started out: 1) every business owner in the complex could greatly benefit from what we had to offer, and 2) for tactical purposes, he might occasionally introduce me as his nephew who recently lost both parents in a head-on collision.

We'd barely begun our mission before finding ourselves seated in the office of the mall manager, where Bob was made to read the uncluttered details of a strict no-solicitation policy. He finished it with a sigh, took off his reading glasses, and sailed the document back across the manager's desk. While he had very little in the way of rebuttal, he did let the man know that he was dear friends with former Pennsylvania lieutenant governor Ernie Kline.

There wasn't much in the way of cold calling after that. Bob took a game swipe at a Hispanic guy in a shoe repair place down the street, but this was ultimately aborted due to "cultural obstacles." It was decided that we needed to regroup, and somehow that brought us to a nearby bowling alley, where Bob downed a beer and I played Q*bert. Leaning against the machine, he kept imploring me to "shoot the little prick," which was not the object of the game. Finally, I explained that Q*bert was a lover not a fighter. That one hit Bob so hard he spit out a mouthful of Stroh's and laughed until he started to choke. "Jesus, Adam, where do you get this shit?" A few beers later, he called it a day and said we'd pick it back up tomorrow.

At home that night, my father asked me how things were going with Dirschberger. I told him it was difficult to tell. Reassuring me, he said, "In this business, you have to start in the gutter and get the shit kicked out of you a little bit. Dirschberger's your man for that. One day, you'll move on and work for a class act like Marty Stump."

Bob was out with the flu for a few days, but he arrived back at the office reenergized and waving a scrap of newspaper. It was an ad for a new tavern in Harrisburg called Totty's Atmo-sphere. Restaurant owners, he asserted, make excellent pros-pects because they skim cash from the bar and need a place to park it. The bullpen didn't stir. Under his breath, I heard Buddy Fowler refer to Bob as "a fiercely dedicated fool." "C'mon, you hotshots," Bob implored, "who wants in on this?" They all played dead. So I raised my hand. Bullshitters.

Roughly two-thirds of the way to Totty's, Bob began to realize the address was "on the hill," referring to Allison Hill, a black neighborhood in Harrisburg that was generally considered unsafe. As the landscape changed around us, Bob muttered with concern, "Where the fuck are we?" His anxi-ety increased after observing some men on a porch playing dominoes. "Jesus," he gasped, "by sundown they'll be lucky to find our toenails."

We finally pulled up to Totty's, and Bob let out a sigh. Through a crack in his window he offered an overly friendly "Hiya, fellas!" to some puzzled teenagers sitting on the curb. Then he turned to me and said in a low voice, "Adam, I can't leave my car on this street unattended. Go in and talk to the owner. You can do it. Just follow the sales book. I'll circle the block until you come out. If there's no sign of you in thirty minutes, I'll call the cavalry." I stepped out of the car and Bob floored it.

I was already sweating as I crossed the street. It had less to do with nerves than the suit I was wearing—a black pinstripe my mom bought me from a markdown place called Cindy's for Men II. It was a decent suit, but not without its quirks; the shiny fabric refused to breathe and always felt moist to the touch, like the skin of sea cow. Additionally, the left lapel tended to pop up without warning, and something sharp, which I was never able to locate or identify, kept jabbing my shoulder blade. Still, it bore the name Pierre Cardin, so who was I to judge?

It was dim and cool inside Totty's Atmosphere. The jukebox glowed yellow through the cigarette smoke like a spacecraft as Stevie Wonder sang "My Cherie Amour." A heavyset woman behind the bar greeted me with "How you doing today, hon?" and set down a wicker basket of Fritos. I've always had a fondness for ladies who call me "hon." I took a seat at the bar and ordered a piece of lemon pie. The woman's name was Larice, and in a short time I learned about her recent kidney operation and the birth of her latest grandchild, met the pastor of her church, and held a smudged picture of her mother in an open casket. There was no way I going to bring up fucking insurance.

Larice took a phone call and I walked over to watch some guys play pool. I had a lot of shit running through my head.

What was wrong with me? Bob was out there circling the block and I had a job to do. I was broke. Most of my friends had jobs or were going to college. My Dodge Colt was hacking up fluids, and there was zero chance I'd ever have sex with that chick who works at Italian Delight.

I walked back to the bar. Unable to look Larice in the eye, I asked her if the owner was in. Soon there was a loud thud as the kitchen doors swung open and a man with one leg rolled out in a wheelchair. I suddenly became aware of the Vietnam War artifacts hanging from the walls. I stood to greet him. He noticed the vinyl binder tucked under my arm and jokingly asked, "You ain't here to sell me nothin', are ya?" I promptly replied, "No." It was just a hunch, but for some reason, I felt he didn't need a refresher course on the uncertainties of life from Adam Resnick.

A moment later I was standing on the curb, flagging down Bob, who had just screeched around the corner. He barely stopped as I jumped in the car.

"It was a bust," I told him. "The guy already has a policy with Mass Mutual." Bob seemed happy just to get out of Dodge as he barreled down the street. "Don't get me wrong," he said, "I love jazz and the rest of it, but ever since Malcolm X, all bets are off." After a long drag on his Carlton, he added, "Mass Mutual's a whorehouse."

I spent the next few months in a haze of cold calls and weak leads, floundering to make a single sale. The traction that allegedly comes to new agents never arrived in my case, and the idea of making a quarter of a million dollars in three years now seemed overly optimistic. I did not possess my father's charisma, his verbal dexterity, or his ability to scare the shit out of people. The idea of me selling insurance was like sending in a pig to perform an angioplasty. (Something I think I saw once on *Green Acres*.)

As my financial anxieties increased, I was forced to take a drastic and unusual step unbecoming of a state-licensed insurance agent: I applied for the six-to-midnight shift at the Uni-Mart on Front Street. Despite my worries, I was not deemed overqualified. I kept the job a secret from Bob, ashamed that I was now making a guaranteed income like those "other slobs." Sure, it was only minimum wage, but I was able to supplement that by stealing. Money tossed on the counter for a quick pack of Winstons became my money. Things like Trac II razors and batteries for my Walkman were no longer a bothersome expense. And postage stamps? What kind of asshole pays for postage stamps?

But how much longer could I go on like this—struggling

to sell insurance by day and embezzling Eskimo Pies at night? I ball-parked it at a decade or two, yet, at the same time, I was beginning to have strange thoughts. Like a dog lurching along the grass, making guttural sounds from its esophagus, gooey, half-digested ideas began to emerge: *Get your ass in gear. Get the fuck out of Harrisburg. Get away from your family. Don't steal more than three lottery tickets per shift.*

Yes, embryonic goals were slowly taking form, but I was still fuzzy on direction. There was only one thing I was sure of (other than the fact that I'd never bang that chick from Italian Delight): I had to quit the insurance business. But how could I leave Bob without having made a single sale? I didn't want him to think it reflected on his training. From bars to bowling alleys to the racetrack, he put in a lot of time with me. He treated me like an adult.

It was after eleven on a slow Thursday night. I was a little tired, so I decided to close forty-five minutes early. I had already locked up and turned off the lights and was in the process of filling a bag with Polaroid film and Mr. Goodbars when I heard the rumble. It was low and powerful and the Tic Tacs on the counter began to chatter in their plastic boxes. I looked out, squinting, as two blazing orbs sailed into the parking lot, bleaching the world white. Then, all at once, there was silence and darkness. A jacked-up '78 Bronco was resting in the handicapped space. The door groaned opened and a large figure emerged. The interior light on the driver's door swept across a pair of black Frye boots with pilgrim buckles.

He approached the store. It was obvious we were closed, but he tried the doors anyway, shaking them so hard a couple of wiffle balls from a nearby display box rolled off and bounced down the aisle. I reached for my keys and haltingly made my way toward the entrance. Our eyes met.

"Hey, man, is that you, Resnick? Lemme grab a pack of Marlboros."

Jeff Glogower had graduated several years ahead of me and was a friend of my older brother Jack. He was a big dude—a typical Perry County mountain man—who played on the football team until getting kicked off for squirting oven cleaner in the face of an opposing quarterback. Since then, he'd found success selling pot, steroids, and select reptiles that were not legal to own.

I comped him a carton of Marlboros and we sat down on the curb next to the ice machine. He smoked and I stared at the river. He asked me what I was up to these days. I explained I was all screwed up, trying to figure shit out. He suggested I sell drugs. I told him I wanted out of sales. The conversation drifted to the erosion of his three-month marriage. The light had long gone out on that relationship, he told me. His liberal use of the term "raging cunt" seemed to confirm this.

"She went and got her ass pregnant," he said. "Now she tells me I can't come near my own goddamn kid."

"That sucks," I responded.

"It's gonna suck a whole lot worse when I shoot her in the fucking eye."

He was just blowing off steam. Perry County guys always talk about killing their wives and girlfriends, but seldom follow through.

"I know that bitch. She'll get herself a lawyer. She'll take my truck, my money, and shack up with some dude who's gonna get his dick sucked on my dime." It was obvious he still loved her.

Suddenly, a dim spark fired somewhere in the depths of my frontal lobe. A connection was made between Jeff's plight and something I had recently kind of learned about. Bam! I asked Jeff if he knew anything about life insurance. He wondered if it was anything like car insurance. I told him yes, it was just like car insurance, only for people.

I was off and running, explaining concepts I barely understood and others I knew nothing about. But the spine of my proposal was solid: I could design a policy for Jeff that ensured the death benefit or any cash value would go exclusively to his son. His ex-wife and whatever dude she might be blowing couldn't touch it. Jeff fell in love with the idea, especially since he felt certain he'd be dead by thirty. He called it his "final 'fuck you' from the grave."

Soon he was filling out sticky, dog-eared paperwork on the hood of his Bronco. I had to fish the forms out of my trunk, where a bloated can of Dad's root beer had exploded. We shook hands on the deal and he thanked me for the smokes.

I had made my first sale. True, my client would eventually require a doctor's exam, which might raise a flag or two, but I wasn't going to fret about that now. I'd accomplished my goal: I could retire from the insurance business with one on the scoreboard.

The following morning, I strode into Dirschberger & Associates with Jeff Glogower's application rolled up in my hand like a degree from Oxford. I wanted Bob to see that his wisdom and leadership had borne fruit before I quit.

I knocked on his door and let myself in. Bob sat alone, gazing quietly at the Pizza Hut across the street. The sun bounced harshly off the red roof, giving his office a Technicolor glow. Had he been wearing a cape, he might have resembled Rhett Butler.

"It's a frightening world we live in, Adam," he finally said. "Things like 'allegiance' and 'loyalty' . . . those are just words these days. We've become small." He swiveled his chair to face me. "They're bringing in a new honcho."

"They're transferring you to another agency?" I replied, shocked.

"They're transferring me to the cemetery. I'm gone."

I told him it didn't make sense, even though it made complete sense. Everything was changing. You could feel it. Places like this and guys like Bob were on borrowed time. Something different was coming—a world where it would be harder to get away with stuff and every battery would be accounted for.

"Nine years," Bob sighed. "This place was a dump when I took it over from Kaplan. Lapsed policies? You could wallpaper your house. The goddamn files were in Chinese. Not one thumbtack. Look anywhere. Thumbtacks were like caviar."

I assured him his mark on the agency would live on. Then I slid Jeff Glogower's application across his desk. "You made a sale?" he said, brightening up. He walked over and crushed me in his arms. I told him it was his sale as much as mine. Then I tendered my resignation. He tried to talk me out of it, but I insisted I couldn't possibly work there without him. Bob admitted I was probably making the right decision. Rumor had it they were replacing him with Len Speece from Doylestown, "a complete fruit."

That night, we returned to the Holiday Inn where we'd

once celebrated my passing the insurance exam. This time I drank. I toasted Bob, who had vowed to open his own financial-estate-planning-consulting something or other. "Everything'll be under one umbrella," he kept saying over and over. "And you'll be my top dog. We'll beat the bastards at their own game."

Later, he struck up a conversation with a middle-aged woman who sat alone at the bar, telling her she had a "smashing figure." It wasn't true, but she accepted the compliment. Neither seemed particularly attracted to the other. Within moments, though, the flicker was back in his eye. As he took her hand and led her to the dance floor, he nudged my ribs and said, "That's all you can do, pal—take it where you can get it."

The Agitator Slat

Fast food, as the saying goes, is shit. The jury came in on that a while ago. Nonetheless, I do find myself indulging from time to time, mostly to keep my ego in check. Only a narcissistic asshole would consider his body a temple.

When the urge hits me for this sort of fare, two things are assured: I'll walk into the restaurant, salivating like a Bernese mountain dog, and exit, feeling like a drug mule with a ruptured condom in his large intestine. But looking back on all the years of hamburgers, Kentucky Fried Chicken, and double-wrapped tacos, I'd have to say the most unhealthy thing I ever consumed, compliments of a national fast-food chain, was a milk shake with a razor blade in it.

This is no urban legend, folks. This is not the woman who claimed her salivary glands became infested with maggots after she ingested unpasteurized honey, or the guy who swore he found a human penis in a box of Rice Chex. What happened to me—this razor blade thing—actually *happened*. It occurred sometime ago at a fast-food restaurant on Ninth Avenue in New York City.

Before I continue, my publisher's legal department, in all their Hebrew fanaticism, has required that I abide by the following:

1. I cannot use the name of the restaurant chain.
2. The words "milk shake" will be substituted for the name of the actual product, which is indeed a milk shake but employs a minor gimmick in an attempt to stand out from other milk shakes.
3. I am prohibited from referencing, no matter how obliquely, a rumored sex-slave scandal involving the chain's upper management. ("And don't try to get cute with little jokes, 'cause I'll burn the whole fucking book"—*unnamed lawyer, via telephone.*)

And now, on with the show!

It was a typical Sunday. I've always hated Sundays. Come

Monday, the shit starts all over again and it goes on like that until they plant you. I stopped into the pint-sized dump I called an office to go over some paperwork and contemplate suicide. Too lazy for the former and too much of a pansy for the latter, I settled on lunch. I decided to dine on the cheap. I wanted something as lousy as I was feeling.

I ordered the special, or as it's known in fast-food parlance, "the combo." In this case, it was combo number 3: cheeseburger, fries, and a drink. "Would you like dessert with that?" I was asked. Pretending it was the goddamnedest proposition I'd ever heard in my life, I let out a resigned sigh and ordered a small chocolate milk shake, emphasizing the word *small* like I was in training for a big bout at the Garden.

A purple neon sign freckled with dead bugs announced DINING ROOM UPSTAIRS. I made the trip and slid into an empty booth. A feeling of shame came over me, similar to those first few moments in a whorehouse parlor when the piano player starts singing "Ol' White Boy's Gonna Get Hisself Some Pussy Tonight Rag."

If you've never been to a fast-food restaurant, envisioning the State Dining Room at Buckingham Palace would be off the mark. To be objective, though, what this place lacked in elegance, it made up for in filth. Before setting my tray down, I used an oven mitt constructed of napkins to clear my table of stray bits of lettuce, orphaned french fries, and a tableau of smeared condiments most likely inspired by Jackson Pollock. All told, the diner before me left enough food behind that with a little ingenuity and a strong stomach, you could create an entirely new meal. Something "off menu."

My burger and fries went down without incident, garnering a rating somewhere between "acceptable" and "what the fuck was I thinking." I'd brought along the *New York Post* to distract me from the particulars of what was going into my mouth, and by the time I got to the milk shake—which was so wonderfully gelatinous I had to eat it with a spoon—I was engrossed in an article about Donald Trump and some beef he had with Leona Helmsley. Just as I started daydreaming about personally brokering the peace between these two American treasures, I felt my spoon scrape the bottom of the cup. I glanced down. That's when I noticed something protruding from the last chocolaty blob of pig collagen. Alarm bells went off in my head as I braced myself for the possibility of vomiting on the guy at the next table. I took a deep breath and tentatively scooped up the whole wad and dumped it into a napkin.

Out of generic convenience, it's easy to lapse into the term "razor blade." But what I discovered wasn't a classic men's shaving blade—the kind you picture nestling beneath the skin of a Halloween apple. This one was narrower and more industrial looking, approximately an inch long and maybe a quarter of an inch wide. It had a little punch hole on one end where a rivet might go and appeared to have broken off from a larger part of something else. It was the "fun size" of razor blades—perfect for swallowing whole while you're distracted, reading a story about a prick billionaire.

I had a hard time wrapping my head around it. What was it doing in a milk shake? Even for a fast-food restaurant, it didn't make sense. A gob of chewing gum? Sure. A Band-Aid? Why not. A back molar? Classic. But a thin little razor blade that could actually kill someone? That's Broadway, baby.

I asked for the manager but was told he was off for the weekend, so I requested to see the highest-ranking employee on duty. A Bunny Wailer–looking dude named Joplin soon appeared on the other side of the counter. Assuming he was about to get the run-of-the-mill bitch about cold french fries or piss on the restroom floor, he was already fingering his pocket for a free medium soda coupon the way a gunslinger reaches for his Colt Rainmaker. Keeping it cool, I wordlessly laid the bunched-up napkin on the counter. Then I dramatically opened it, exposing the blade like a freshwater pearl.

"I just found that in my milk shake," I pronounced, trying

to sound like a cross between Steven Seagal and Morley Safer. Joplin reached down and picked up the blade. He inspected it for a moment and shook his head.

"There's no way this came from my milk shake machine," he stated definitively in a Caribbean accent. There wasn't a hint of concern or curiosity in his voice. Instead, his tone seemed to imply that I was up to some kind of monkey business.

"Well . . . it came from *somewhere*," I said. "*I* certainly didn't put it there." My voice quivered a bit. I was born feeling guilty, so it doesn't take much for me to question myself. In this case, though, I felt pretty sure my hands were clean.

"Imagine if a kid got that milk shake?" I continued, growing outraged. "I mean, someone could've died from this thing."

He looked at the blade again, exhaled, and disappeared for a moment. He returned with a stubby pencil and a fresh napkin and told me to write down my name and phone number. Obviously Joplin wasn't going to expend much energy on this one. It was a departure from the norm, and they don't pay him for shit like that. He told me he'd show the blade to his manager on Monday, and if the manager felt it warranted further investigation, he'd send it off to "corp."

"Do you promise me you'll do that?" I asked, unintentionally sounding like the boss man on a sugar plantation.

"What did I say to you?" Joplin snapped. "If I say I'll do it, I'll do it."

He was getting a little grumpy, so I decided to back off, but I told him I'd be stopping by in a few days to follow up. He gave me a smirky nod, as if to convey the Jamaican equivalent of "Oh, goodie, I can't wait."

I was convinced the entire matter would disappear once my shoe hit the sidewalk. The evidence was no longer in my possession. Cell phone cameras were something new in those days, and I didn't have one. And even if Joplin, who clearly wasn't a fan of mine, showed the blade to his manager, there would be no upside for the guy to take it any further. It was found in *his* location in one of *his* milk shakes. The jagoffs from corp would be all over him like lime aftershave on Donald Trump (sorry to bring him back into it). No, the razor, the napkin, and the whole incident were headed straight for the garbage with the rest of the stink. I'm not a cynic; I'm a realist. Especially when it comes to human beings in positions of power and the dirty business of fast food.

I began having dreams about coughing up blood. I saw diners screaming and knocking over tables to get away from me. I saw the floating head of Leona Helmsley licking red spittle from her Joker smile. Then I was harvesting sugarcane in the oppressive Kingston heat as Joplin whipped me with a riding crop. I sassed him and he threw me in "the box," where I sweated it out with a blind girl I glanced at once in the subway. My hand found its way up her skirt and I was compelled to ask in a flustered voice, "Wait, you are a *girl*, aren't you?" She just laughed and told me to look in my hand. When I opened it, I found two eyeballs. So, sort of a happy ending.

I went back to the restaurant to check on the status of the investigation. Joplin no longer worked there. All I could get out of the young woman behind the counter was that he was "probably in Queens." The manager I spoke to, a friendly middle-aged man with braces on his teeth and a William Holden hairline, knew nothing of the incident. He'd been out for a couple of months with shingles and told me Joplin most likely dealt with the "temp manager." When I asked him if he knew where the temp manager was, he responded, "Not really. Those temps, you know, they kinda float around. I'd say your best bet is Queens."

It was a sufficiently half-assed answer that left me little room to maneuver. For my own peace of mind, though, I had one final question: Had he, at any time during his employment at the restaurant, received complaints from customers who'd encountered razor blades in their milk shakes?

He crinkled his eyes and appeared to search his memory. "No," he finally chuckled, "I think I'd remember something like that." Then he added, "A lady fished a moth out of her coffee once, but that had more to do with the fluorescents."

I moved on with my life. The milk shake, the razor blade,

Joplin, Bill Holden, and the blind girl—I put it all behind me. The bad dreams had subsided, replaced with new ones that involved more fucking and less blood.

Approximately six weeks later, my phone rang. A polite-sounding woman with a light Southern accent inquired, "Is this Mr. Resnick? Mr. Adam Resnick?" I assumed it was the cable company confirming yet another appointment to determine why the bedroom TV keeps freezing up on the Reel-zChannel. She verified my identity and continued.

"This is Mitzi Kurstetter [not her real name] calling from Rumblenuts Corporate [not the actual restaurant chain], following up on the piece of metal you chanced upon in your milk shake at one of our midtown Manhattan locations?"

"Yes?" I answered in astonishment.

"I'd just like to inform you that our engineers have determined that the object did indeed come from the milk shake machine and they are resolving the problem and we apologize for any inconvenience and would like to send you something if I may get your address, sir, please."

It was a rush of information and, I'm fairly certain, a run-on sentence, but I got the gist.

My immediate thoughts were of Joplin and the temp manager. Despite all of my doubts, they *had* done their jobs. I felt like a real shithead. Maybe I was a cynic after all. Perhaps I needed to question my long-held belief that, as a rule, human beings are lazy and incompetent. But then I remembered the the guy who okayed the launch of the *Challenger chicago* I decided to put a pin in it.

My second thought was: *Hold on, sister. Not so fast. That razzle-dazzle might have worked with the moth lady, but now you're talking to someone with half a brain.* I wanted answers and no amount of Southern-fried double-talk was going to stop me.

"For my own sanity," I began, "please explain to me why a razor blade—or as you call it, an 'object'—is necessary or even helpful in the preparation of a milk shake?"

"Thank you for that question, sir. Technically, the name of the part is an agitator slat, which helps create texture uniformity during the mixing process, and I can assure you, our franchisees have been notified of the incident and will do the necessary equipment checks to ensure this piece of apparatus remains secure in the future and I would so appreciate your address, Mr. Resnick, *sir*."

Boy, she was good. My lungs hurt just from listening to her. I changed my strategy. Instead of grilling her, I'd give her some real words to chew on.

"I mean, thank God it was me and not a little kid. I have a young daughter. Thank God she didn't go along with me. She eats a lot of crap, not that we encourage it, but it's very likely she would've asked for a milk shake if she'd gone along with me. And I can assure you, this call would be quite a bit different if that were the case. As it would be for all families."

A brief silence.

"May I get your address, please, sir?"

When the call ended, I felt like I'd been run over by a truck. But then it suddenly sunk in: Rumblenuts Corp was sending me something.

Lorrie and I discussed it over dinner. What could it be? She predicted anything from a formal apology to a couple of grand. Meanwhile, I had it from a good source that her mother was telling everyone I was a "gigantic asshole" for not "going after their wallets."

As the days wore on, I tried not to think about it, but my brain had other ideas. Finally, about a week after the call from Ms. Kurstetter, an envelope arrived, and I tore into that fucker like an ape skins a plantain.

Inside was a wallet-sized cardboard folder with the restaurant's colorful logo. I cracked it open, and there, staring up at me, safely tucked into four small slots to keep it in place, was a Rumblenuts gift card for forty dollars. Printed inside the folder were the words "Enjoy with our compliments at any of our 8,000 restaurants nationwide."

I didn't know what to expect, but I certainly didn't expect *this*. Gift cards are what franchisees pass out to Cub Scouts for picking up litter or nudging junkies to homeless shelters—

the whole "we're part of the community" jazz. Not that I was expecting a payday, but considering the circumstances, I anticipated something a little more personal. Perhaps a Rumblenuts Certificate of Merit:

In praise of Adam Resnick, who alerted us to a potentially deadly situation rather than running like a bitch to a lawyer or the local pennysaver.

But what I really struggled with was the awkward amount. Forty dollars. It wasn't just that it was cheap; it was uniquely cheap. There had to be some thought behind it. Were they trying to send me a message? Had it been in error? Or did it have something to do, perhaps, with biblical numerics?

I found myself spending an inordinate amount of time trying to decode the logic and motivation behind the forty-dollar gift card. I probably put as much thought into it as Robert Ballard and the French-American expedition did in finding the *Titanic*. Eventually, though, I calmed down and settled on what I believed to be a plausible scenario.

Please now, allow me to share it with you—minus the tedious repetition of words like "debris field" and "rusticles."

Could someone dim the houselights, please?

Inside a large conference room filled with polished wood and green leather, a cadre of fast-food executives sits around a long oak table with hand-carved legs that was once used by James Madison to draft a portion of the Virginia Resolution.

CEO: Let me understand this: I told you turds a year ago to get a foothold in Angola, and now you come back and say you built ten joints in Angola, Indiana?

EXECUTIVE #1: We're in the process of finding out what happened, sir.

CEO: Goddamn it, I said Africa! Deepest, darkest Africa! Ten years from now they'll have more burger joints than shrunken heads and we'll be sitting here with our nuts in a Dixie cup.

EXECUTIVE #2: We've begun collecting data on factors such as instability in the region and, uh, what kind of stuff they eat. . . .

CEO: Come on, man. These are people who eat fungi and drink water with piss in it. We'll be welcomed like kings.

An assistant furiously scribbles notes on a legal pad.

CEO *(glancing at his watch)*: Okay, what's next? I got a suckjob penciled in for eleven-thirty.

EXECUTIVE #3 *(nervously)*: Well, sir, there was a little something, a sort of incident that occurred at one of our Manhattan restaurants—

CEO: Not interested. Deal with the franchisee. He bought the barn, he can muck it out.

EXECUTIVE #3: Unfortunately, it's not that simple. Uh . . . (*Glances at another executive.*) Jim?

Jim, a solid company man who's spent the past thirty years hiding in his office, stands up, holding a small plastic bag.

CEO: Whadda ya got there, Tutankhamun?

JIM: Sir, this is a razor blade—a piece of a razor blade, actually—that a customer found in his milk shake at the New York location . . .

CEO (*laughs*): Oh, he found it, did he? I'll tell you where he found it—in aisle nine over at Kresge's. Come on, man, this shakedown's older than Moby-Dick.

JIM: If only that were the case. It seems the blade is actually part of a mechanism inside the machine that somehow broke off during the mixing process and, well, found its way into the customer's cup.

CEO: Jesus Christ, they'll padlock this whole taffy box! How many dead?

EXECUTIVE #4: No one. The man who discovered it wasn't injured.

CEO: Have we made plans to kill him?

EXECUTIVE #5: With all due respect, sir, after the little mess we had in Sacramento last year, we felt it best to explore a more cautious solution.

CEO: Goddamn it! I'm sick and tired of being extorted by these cross-eyed Eskimos every time they find a geegaw in their applesauce. Do they think they're chowing at 21? When you walk into a toilet, expect some shit.

EXECUTIVE #6: The good news is, the man who found the blade doesn't seem to be looking for money. We've tapped his phone, monitored his email, one of our operatives has already fucked his wife. There's no indication we're looking at trouble here.

EXECUTIVE #7: None whatsoever.

EXECUTIVE #6: Great point, Bill. I'll let you take it from here.

Bill throws Executive #6 a dirty look and rises reluctantly.

BILL *(addressing the CEO)*: Sir, after consulting with legal, PR, and Father Sweeney—who was kind enough to accept a retainer in case he's needed to make a statement on our behalf—it was determined that if news of this little . . . flub . . . ever leaked to the press, the fallout would be short-lived but costly.

EXECUTIVE #8: The brand is fairly bulletproof at this point, but if customers start fretting about their food pipes getting sliced open . . . well, I just don't think we want to be there. Ken, you wanna hop in?

Perspiring heavily, Ken, a blimplike executive with diabetes, throws a lit cigarette lighter at Executive #8. Gripping the table for support, he makes it unsteadily to his feet.

KEN *(to the CEO)*: Sir, we feel that under the circumstances, since the customer isn't looking to sue us, we should . . . well, there's no other way to say it really . . . compensate him.

CEO *(glowering at Ken)*: Come again, Topsy? The guy's not asking for money, but you want to give him money?

KEN: If he accepts it, I'm told, then we have something on him, but I'm a little fuzzy on . . .

EXECUTIVE #8: It means the guy can't yap. *(To Ken)* Thanks for nothing.

CEO: For crying out loud, people. Kill this razor blade son of a bitch! Burn his house down. Kill his whole fucking family and the goddamn cockatiel. *(Pointing to Ken)* Send blubber-butt down to do it.

Ken faints, hitting his head on the table on the way down. Another exec, Brian, stands up.

BRIAN: We're not talking about a significant sum of money, sir. From what we gather, this particular individual isn't very bright. Rather than approach it as a settlement, we feel we can get away with sending him a modest check . . . as a kind of a thank-you. No wrongdoing implied.

CEO: What are we talking?

EXECUTIVE #9: In the neighborhood of two hundred and fifty thousand.

CEO: That's what you call saving me money?

EXECUTIVE #9: If word of the incident ever became public, the net loss to the company would far exceed—

CEO: No way. Huh-uh. Go Sacramento on this prick.

The room goes silent for several moments.

EXECUTIVE #10: Well, there is one other possibility, something Rusty came up with, but it's a bit unusual, and I certainly don't endorse it unless it works.

The other executives quickly murmur in agreement.

CEO: Who the hell is Rusty?

All eyes fall on Rusty, a young, puny, bright-eyed junior executive who until recently had been an intern in charge of the supply closet.

RUSTY *(looking surprised)*: Gee, I, uh, wasn't prepared for this, but . . . oh boy . . . here goes nothin'.

He's quickly on his feet and starts pacing the boardroom like an old Kentucky trial lawyer who grew up in Brooklyn.

RUSTY: Maybe I'm a little old-fashioned, gentlemen, but the way I see it, if a man's shopping for a horse, you don't throw in the stable. This fella in New York only wants one thing: to feel good about himself. He's a nobody, a schlub. He's dying to be a hero just once in his life. So I say we give him that. We say, ah, "Thanks for pointing out the issue, pal, we got it all locked down. You're a saint, a regular Clark Kent. Here's a little something for not wasting too much of our time." Then we toss him back in the lake with the rest of the carp.

CEO: What do you call "a little something," son?

Rusty grins.

RUSTY: Not money. Not a check. Not even a savings bond for little Scotty's trade school jar. What we give him is . . .

Long pause.

RUSTY: . . . a gift card.

General grumbling in the room.

RUSTY: Because that's how nice we are at Rumble-nuts. Even though our product is virtually priceless, and its quality so high that scientists have yet to devise a way to measure it, we're willing to share some of that treasure with him. Because our food is not fast, it's not shit, and it's not sharp. It's gold. And that's what he gets for the privilege of complaining to us.

Rusty sighs and shrugs his shoulders.

RUSTY: But, hey, what do I know? I'm green as grass.

CEO *(cracking a smile for the first time)*: And, uh . . . Rusty, is it? Exactly how large a gift card are we talking about?

EXECUTIVE #11 *(suddenly hopping on board)*: A hundred dollars! Ha-ha! And not a penny more!

RUSTY: Too high.

EXECUTIVE #12: Rusty's right! Twenty-five dollars!

RUSTY: Too low.

EXECUTIVE #12: Fifty clams and we put it to bed!

RUSTY: Too logical.

CEO *(fascinated)*: How much do you think it should be, Rusty?

Rusty walks over to a large mahogany-framed chalkboard and starts to write down a figure. The CEO and the executives are on the edge of their seats. Finally Rusty steps aside, revealing the number 0. There's a collective gasp in the room. Rusty laughs.

RUSTY: Come on, guys. It's a gag.

He puts a four in front of the zero.

CEO: It's glorious! It's magnificent! *(Beat)* But, Rusty, it's a very unusual number, don't you think?

RUSTY: Yes it is, sir. And that's precisely what we want. Something bold yet mysterious. Clear-cut yet confusing. Well-intentioned but obnoxious. Something that not only melts the brain but also has the ability to, dare I say, *hypnotize.*

He waves his hand through the air like an illusionist. The other executives trail it with glazed eyes.

CEO: Do you think this fellow in New York'll go for it?

RUSTY: We just need to soften him up first, with a little courtesy, a little professionalism . . . and a whiff of magnolia.

A few minutes later, the executives and the CEO are huddled around Mitzi Kurstetter, a buxom, poof-haired blond bombshell from the secretarial pool who also happens to be Rusty's sweetheart. She sits at the conference table, holding a telephone receiver and reading from a prepared script Rusty has provided.

"Mr. Resnick? This is Mitzi Kurstetter calling from Rumblenuts Corporate, following up on the piece of metal you chanced upon in your milk shake . . ."

The call plays out. When it's over, a tape recorder attached to the telephone is clicked off and the executives cheer Mitzi's performance as well as her ass and blow job lips. The CEO claps Rusty on the back.

CEO: How would you and your lady friend like to join me at the club for brunch this weekend?

RUSTY: Gee, it'd be a great honor, sir.

The meeting disperses; the other executives pat Rusty on the shoulder on their way out. Rusty picks Mitzi up and twirls her around, saying, "I'm on my way to the stars, baby. And you're coming along to wax the rocket." Mitzi becomes too heavy for him. Winded, he lays her down on the floor.

If life is indeed a series of familiar scenes and passages, I still don't get the razor blade thing. Was it a big deal, or just a forty-dollar deal? What if I had saved another person's life— a child's, perhaps—simply by being in the right place at the right time? Maybe that's the sole reason I was put on earth. To take the milk shake for the other guy.

Anyway, that's what I keep telling myself.

Curtain.

The Porter's Screenplay

The nine steps I take each morning from my apartment door to the elevator occur unconsciously and in a bubble. I push the button and wait as the same mantra fills my head, ticking off like a jittery second hand on a cheap watch. *I'm a disaster. I'm a lazy piece of shit. I deserve everything bad that happens to me. I'm not worthy of anyone's respect. I should go blow some money. I don't deserve to blow money. I'm not in the position to blow money. Fuck everyone. Ah, the sound of lapping waves. The ocean. Calming. Reassuring. I'm drowning. The undertow is sucking me under . . .*

Francisco, the porter, is sloshing the mop across the tile floor in the hallway, leaving a trail of gray sudsy water. Latin music leaks from his headphones. Up-tempo, alive, foreign, awful. We stand there together every morning. Our conversation is a ritual that neither of us tampers with. It goes something like this:

"Hey, Francisco."

"Morning, sir."

"Hot out there?"

"Yeah, they say it rains today and it's gonna cool everything off."

"That's good. We could use a little rain." The elevator arrives. "Okay, see you later." And I'm gone.

This is my idea of a perfect conversation. Why can't all human interaction be like this? God bless Francisco. He gets it.

On one particular morning, however, something was out of whack. I glanced up at the elevator indicator and it was motionless: frozen on B—that subterranean no-man's-land with washing machines, garbage cans, and a mysterious locker my wife refers to when she goes down to retrieve our Christmas decorations. Francisco kills the salsa.

"It's coming in a minute. Hector's fixing the lapper," he told me. I don't know what a lapper is or if I even heard it correctly, but clearly Francisco and I were going to have a larger space to fill today. I retreated back into my head. *I'm so sick of Multi-Grain Cheerios. Why does she keep buy-*

ing it? I told her to stop buying it. Everything's a subtle "fuck you." Except for the times when it's not so subtle. I deserve it all. I'm a nightmare. I wonder what it feels like to save a child's life? The grateful mother embracing me and sobbing into my chest . . . the family inviting me over for a special dinner . . . my reluctant speech at the church service held in my honor where I tell the congregation, "I'm not a hero. God is the hero."

Francisco: "You stay busy these days?"

The words came at me like a swarm of yellow jackets.

"Uh, yeah, trying to. Ha-ha. How about you?"

He ignored my question.

"You write for the movies? I saw your name one night, I think it was on Starz."

I cringed.

"Yeah, sometimes."

Francisco: "I forget the movie. On Starz."

"I'm sure it wasn't very good, whatever it was. Ha-ha."

Francisco: "Right. It was kind of trying to be something, but . . ."

My stomach churned. I glanced at the elevator.

Francisco: "I buy a lot of movies, you know, from Best Buy? *Blair Witch, Crouching Tiger, Shawshank . . .*"

The elevator indicator was now fossilized and appeared fused to the dial.

". . . *Seabiscuit, Chicken Run, Thelma and Louise . . .*"

My eyes found the stairwell. Only ten flights down. After all, this was a fire. But it would be insulting—like I was trying to get away from him. I'd obsess and feel guilty about it for weeks. I stayed put. He continued to rattle off movie titles, crescendoing with *The Passion of the Christ* and the *Rush Hour* troika. *Chin up*, I thought. *The worst is over.*

Francisco: "Is it hard to write a movie?"

I was fucked.

"I mean, do you just make up the words?"

"Well, yeah, you have to kind of figure it out," I heard myself say.

Like the rumble of an approaching express train, I knew what was coming.

Francisco: "'Cause I have, like, seven or eight movies I want to write."

A chunk of my cranium blew out and sailed through the air. Sadly, I was still alive.

"Really? Wow. That's a lot."

Francisco: "The first one is about a ghost. Did you ever see *Super Size Me*?"

I struggled to connect the dots.

"Yes, I've seen it."

Francisco: "Okay, so this is like *Super Size Me*, but the man dies. My wife doesn't like regular scary movies. She likes paranormal."

I jabbed the elevator button five times in rapid succession, fully aware it would accomplish nothing.

Francisco: "So I'm going to write that one first. How long does a movie script have to be? How many pages?"

"It depends. Roughly a hundred and twenty."

Francisco: "Well, this will be shorter. Maybe sixteen pages. What kind of paper should I use?"

I felt like I'd been injected with a powerful drug meant for cattle. "Uh . . . just regular printer paper," I replied.

Francisco: "Yeah, I think I'll just write it in a notebook."

"Yup, do that," I instantly agreed. He could have said he was writing it on the shell of a Chinese box turtle and I would've given him my blessing.

Suddenly, the sound of whirring. A slow whoosh. Creaking. The indicator was moving. *It's coming!*

Francisco: "'Cause I want it to be good."

"Of course."

"I want it to *be* something."

"I don't blame you."

"And then maybe you can tell me where to send it. Maybe to Starz."

"Absolutely."

The elevator door opened. I propelled myself inside.

"Okay, well, good luck with everything, Francisco."

I gently depressed the DOOR CLOSE button, trying not to be obvious.

"Mr. Resnick!"

The door started to close, scraping across the metal track.

"Yes?"

I watched as the wood panel slowly wiped him from view. In the final moment, only a sliver of Francisco remained. It was all he needed.

"Does it have to be in English?"

Boy 6

Note: For the sake of my mental health, the names of my brothers have been omitted and my phone will remain off the hook.

Dark clouds rolled across Beaufort Farms that day, turning the neighborhood into a cluster of shadows. Trees and lawns drained of color as a dusty wind picked up, rattling screen doors like an intruder. The neighbor ladies emerged from their houses, aprons fluttering, and dabbing at their eyes. Again they asked themselves, *How could this happen?* Their prayers had not only gone unanswered; they had been mocked. My mother was a woman of almost unearthly kindness and did not deserve such a fate. They looked toward Orchard Hill Road as my father's car crested the summit and then disappeared down the steep driveway leading to the woodsy pit of land where our house stood. The ladies slowly walked back to their homes, dazed and muttering, aware that a measure of their faith would depart forever with the storm. This was the afternoon Joyce came home from the hospital with my twin brothers.

There were already four of us Resnick boys, which was four more than the world ever needed. When my mother became pregnant for the final time, a collective cry echoed throughout Susquehanna Township: *Please, let it be a girl.* No one could have imagined a fifth, let alone *sixth* boy. Nor could they have fathomed the horrible, jangly mass of energy that had just been unleashed down in that pit. The monster was now complete. I was five years old and wholly unprepared for the cyclone of madness and testosterone that would shape me into the nervous wreck I am today.

It would be inadequate to portray Merv's reaction to the arrival of his new sons as mere fatherly pride; what he displayed was more like a profound and lofty arrogance. His magnificent balls had been set on this planet to produce *males*. It was as if nature itself, in all its ferocity, had chiseled two more glorious chunks from a monolithic rock, transforming his usual swagger into a one-man procession that announced to the neighborhood fathers, "Outta my way, faggots. Go pick some cherries." Yet, in the midst of this gloating, a curious omen appeared: the custom license plate he'd ordered for my mother's station wagon had arrived botched, trumpeting BOY 6 instead of 6 BOYS. BOY 6 sounded like a code name for a destructive compound accidentally produced in a government laboratory. No one picked up on the significance at the time, but as we know from history, prophecy is often recognized in hindsight.

There were the twins, myself, and the three older ones. It would be unwise of me to identify or categorize beyond that. I will note, however, that 90 percent of the trouble came from the top half of the brood, whose callous savagery existed without wit or deliberation. Collectively, the brothers formed a nebulous blob that oozed and pulsated throughout my youth, creating a psychological house of horrors that still leaves me drenched in sweat in the hush of night.

The adolescent years in Resnickland might have passed for a quaint *Little Rascals* two-reeler, with its misplaced amphibians hopping through my mother's kitchen, firecrackers set alight in school lavatories, and stolen horse corn peddled by the roadside to suckers on their way home for dinner. Good old Huck Finn mischief-making in an age when kids were seen as pests rather than influential consumers. But as the elder brothers entered their teens, things deteriorated quickly and chaotically, producing a toxic hellhole of insolence, hostility, and freshly fucked hippie chicks smuggled out of second-floor windows on Sunday mornings by knotted bedsheets. The youthful bond between the brothers frayed and sparked, replaced by shifting alliances and checkerboard grudges, secrets and snitches, cruel jokes and disproportionate vengeance. There was no undertone of sibling rivalry or Oedipal muck; that was too highfalutin for the Resnick boys. We kept things bracingly simple: when the dust settled, no one really liked each other. And my heart never stopped racing. The enemy could be sitting right across the dinner table.

Two things always struck me when visiting another person's home: the civil tone in which family members spoke to one another and the sight of open doors. The latter implied trust, a concept that was as fanciful to me as the Batmobile. Thievery was rampant in the Resnick house, and every brother, at a certain age, installed a padlock on his bedroom door, leaving the upstairs hallway looking like a corridor in a storage facility. Most of the theft came at the hand of one particular brother who pillaged his way through our belongings with the quiet efficiency of airborne bacteria. Money was his preference, but he was content to steal anything that could be flipped for cigarettes, *Penthouse* magazines, Tastykakes, or other life-sustaining provisions. A framed collection of rare buffalo nickels passed down from my grandfather was dismantled and used to purchase a carton of orangeade. Angelfish from our aquarium were jarred and swapped with a neighbor boy for a copy of *Hole* magazine, a publication that, I can assure you, had little to do with golf. He once found a twenty-dollar bill

I had hidden in the hollow leg of a Frankenstein model, and replaced it with a note that said, "Nice try, dumb fuck." See, it wasn't enough to just *steal*; you had to be a prick about it too.

As it was, I was born nervous—a condition built into me the way brake lights come standard on cars. But even in the relative safety of my bedroom, behind a locked door fortified by a blanket chest stacked with dumbbells, it was impossible to relax. Physical barriers offered little protection against mental assault, and my privacy was routinely invaded in imaginative and horrific ways. One brother had a KGB-like obsession with the personal affairs of family members that kept the entire house on edge. I remember the chill that ran down my spine one evening as I passed his bedroom and heard the sound of my own laughter seeping through the door. It was second nature to presume my phone calls were being surveilled by someone on the premises, but in the depths of my paranoia I could not have imagined they were being recorded and archived. The unique experience of eavesdropping on yourself is not a pleasant one, made even more unsettling when hearing a mundane conversation long forgotten. Adding to the creep-fest was my brother's compulsive rewinding and replaying of one particular word from the same snippet of conversation:

ME: "The front of his dad's car got totally fucked up."

GIRL (*chuckling*): "Well, that's what he gets."

ME (*laughing*): "Imagine that big head of his banging into the steering wheel . . . *CRACK!*"

Stop. Rewind.

"*CRACK!*" Rewind. "*CRACK!*" Rewind. "*CRACK!*" The more I heard it, the more repulsed I became by the sound of my own voice. It was phony and animated, and sounded like a guy I would hate. No wonder nothing ever happened with that girl.

"*CRACK!*"

Why the sick fuck kept playing it over and over is anyone's guess. "*CRACK!*" He had no idea I was even listening. "*CRACK!*" No matter, my lifelong phobia of talking on the telephone had begun. Just another piece of shrapnel for the ol' brain. (Side note: It was eventually discovered this brother had a hidden recording device wired down in the basement that engaged the moment anyone in the house picked up the receiver. When my father confronted him with the apparatus, he claimed it was for a science project, later changing it to a sociology paper on "interrelationships and communication." My dad smashed the tape recorder with a hammer, and the other brothers lined up, demanding "their tapes.")

The only sheriff in town was my father, who worked his ass off every day to keep the cupboards stocked with Apple Jacks and Ken-L Ration. He wisely left the house early and came home late. I always admired him for coming home at all. But when he was around, you could hear a pin drop. Merv was the only living creature the brothers feared. All he had to do was raise his ass an inch from the kitchen chair, and we'd scatter like roaches. He was both slayer and dragon. Yet even he had limitations; he could beat back the vermin, but no man can defeat bubonic plague. Joyce, on the other hand, was on the front line, all day, every day. She saw real action, most of which she kept to herself so the old man wouldn't kill one of us or drop dead of a heart attack. She endured the calls from school, the shoplifting, the altercations, the drugs, the pregnant girlfriends. This woman was an angel, a gentle and compassionate soul admired by everyone who knew her, but she was forced into battle by the unimaginable behavior of her very offspring. How sad to see the startled look on her face when an alien voice leaped from her throat, ordering her loathsome sons to "shut your goddamn mouths and get out!"

Like Lon Chaney Jr. bitten by a werewolf, I, too, transformed into a Resnick beast over time, becoming short-tempered and hostile. By my early teens I was taking my frustrations out on the neighborhood, vandalizing property late at night with some trashy kids from Bell Manor. We destroyed toolsheds, decapitated lawn jockeys, and made pornographic adjustments to Nativity scenes. As was their wont, the Bell Manor gang often capped off the evening by taking a dump in a birdbath or some other hapless receptacle. It's worth noting that these were the waning days of milk boxes. It was all adolescent hijinks, but I felt real anger during these raids. Everyone else was laughing, but in my mind I was settling a score. With whom, I wasn't sure. I certainly had nothing against the guy with the birdbath. The *Clockwork Orange* period ended one night with the inevitable ride to the police station. When my father learned that some of the other kids had beer, my new name around the house became "that fucking drunk."

Unlike most of my brothers I possessed something called a conscience that prevented me from following too closely in their sociopathic footsteps. For me, all it took was a little reflection to feel bad about inverting someone's patio umbrella. But I had to be cautious about getting too soft. The ever-present threat of violence in the house required me to inhabit a perpetual state of readiness. It was not uncommon for a brawl to erupt over the most negligible circumstance. Brother #2 might enter a room wearing a sweatshirt owned by brother #3 and suddenly the shit was flying. Saltshakers, chairs, telephones—if it wasn't nailed down it was ripped out. Dogs would flee the area, ears down and tails tucked, as my mother bravely tried to quash the maelstrom without catching an elbow. Invariably, the defeated brother would end up on the floor, wheezing, bright red, and exhibiting marks on his neck where strangulation had been attempted. Bloodcurdling threats of vengeance would bellow through the house and escape through the screen door, rolling like a dust cloud into neighboring yards, where happy families enjoying a game of Frisbee were treated to the echoes of "You're fucking dead, you cocksucker!"

The thing that separated the Resnick boys from other siblings who got into the occasional fracas was we literally fought to kill. I recall an episode that occurred when I was fourteen in which a brother teased me so ruthlessly about a bad haircut that I went after him with a kitchen knife. Promptly realizing he had no fear of me (he was a bulky bastard and quick to anger when challenged), the hunter became the hunted, and I swiftly retreated. Dropping the knife, I flew up one set of stairs and down another, only to be greeted by another brother who kindly offered his assistance: "Adam," he said in a benevolent tone, "if you'd like a gun, look in the third drawer of my dresser."

So, let's freeze this picture for a moment. Let's suspend lunatic brother #1 as he rounds the corner to kick the fuck out of me, and push in on my bewildered face as I absorb the sales pitch of lunatic brother #2. Did he really have a gun in his dresser? Possibly. Nothing could be ruled out in Resnickland. Still, let's really analyze the scenario, just for shits and giggles.

Assuming brother #2's offer was legit—which I'd put at fifty-fifty—he was proposing the following:

1. He would supply me with a firearm, so I might thereby . . .
2. kill brother #1, which would surely lead to . . .
3. my incarceration and resulting suicide.

Unfreeze.

The chase continued as I sprinted past a German shepherd cowering in the fireplace and out the front door, scurrying into the woods like a pheasant at the sound of buckshot. Luckily, speed trumped size that day and allowed me to reach safety. Through the foliage I could hear a panting voice in the distance—"You're fucking dead, you cocksucker!"

For reasons I assume are obvious, I was in no particular hurry to return home that day. I stayed in the woods for hours, perched on a pile of moist leaves and collecting my thoughts. If events had gone a shade differently, would I have been capable of using that knife? When I grabbed it in a blind rage, I certainly felt committed—justified, even. *Multiple stab wounds to the chest and abdomen.* Just a few keystrokes of the coroner's typewriter. I fished a bent Tareyton from my pocket. I had been trying to learn to smoke and chose this brand for its much ballyhooed charcoal filter, figuring it might taste something like barbecue. *How many more years of this could I take?* I wondered. How would I survive? I fixed my eyes on the bark pattern of a walnut tree. Soon there were visions of setting the woods ablaze and a rolling fireball that flared and expanded, engulfing my house, the neighborhood, and my school. I snapped out of it when I realized my pants were soaked through from the wet leaves. Seething, I took the glowing tip of the cigarette and burned an ant.

Not then, not now, can I fully understand what motivated the behavior at the house off Orchard Hill Road. It was a revolution with no stance or purpose—a cockeyed flag lofted high by sadistic brutes. And in its shadow, I grew like a blighted sapling: stunted, half-rotted, and trembling in the wind, until, at last, I was freed by nothing more dramatic than legal age. I had spent nearly two decades barricaded inside my bedroom, daydreaming about my escape, only to limp off like a raccoon dragging a claw trap on its hind leg.

And so, there came to be another time, a time when my wife became pregnant with what would be our first and only child. I went into a kind of a tailspin when I heard the news, and a vulgar prayer bubbled up from the pit of my acid-filled stomach: "Please, God, not a boy." I could not bear the thought of bringing another Resnick male into the world—or, even more alarming, into my home. My obsession for a girl consumed me, and with it came incredible guilt at the notion that I was rejecting a possible son before he was born. What kind of emotional damage was I already inflicting on him? This was sure to be the most fucked-up Resnick boy in history. Lorrie attempted good old-fashioned reasoning, assuring me I would find it impossible not to love my own child, regardless of gender. If it wound up being a son, it would be *our* son—not the dreaded "seventh Resnick brother" of my nightmares. I tried to take comfort in this, but as the creature inside her belly grew, I recognized something in those spastic kicks. They were crazed and full of hostility. The Hydra was forming, a ghastly five-headed boy-beast possessing the worst characteristics of each of my siblings. It was coming, unbridled and unrestrained, to blot out the sun, destroy my life, and record my phone calls.

As Lorrie's second trimester passed into the third, and my anxieties continued unabated, she finally conveyed that I was an "asshole" and "fucked in the head" and had "better get some fucking help" because she wasn't putting up with my "psycho bullshit" anymore.

In her own sweet way, she was suggesting I engage the services of a therapist or some other like-minded sorcerer. Unfortunately, the Resnick male didn't believe in limp-wristed philosophies like "self-improvement." Shrinks were for weaklings and invertebrate Jews with too much money on their hands. No, a provocative step like psychiatry would have to wait for some larger crisis, like dealing with a terminal illness or being raped in the woods by hillbillies during a canoe trip with my buddies. Instead, I decided to seek wisdom from the source, the figurative Play-Doh Fun Factory that extruded this whole mess in the first place: my mother.

I journeyed back to Harrisburg and sat across from Joyce at the Excellent Inn, an ironically named slophouse facing the brown-foamed banks of the Susquehanna. "I don't remember you boys being so bad," she said, stirring a cup of coffee. I clarified: "Well, *I* wasn't so bad. I was out of my mind, but I wasn't malicious like most of the others."

"Well, all kids have their little quirks. You'll see once you have your own."

I felt the need to refresh her memory a bit. Did she recall the son who had a cute habit of visiting my aunt Sarah once a month and forging her Social Security checks? Or the other son who, out of sheer laziness, liked to piss out his bedroom window in the middle of the night, hitting the ledge below before backspraying onto the kitchen table? And what about the boy who, at the tender age of nineteen, went into a rage and threw a Pepsi bottle at me when the TV went out in the middle of *The Wizard of Oz*? Did she recall the shard of glass that embedded itself in my cheek, barely missing my eye?

I looked down and noticed the coffee cup I was gripping rattling on its saucer.

Always one to look on the bright side, my mother responded, "At least none of you were like the Peifer boy. Remember him? Always leaving strange things in the mailbox?"

"But he was legitimately schizophrenic," I protested. "I'm talking about cruel, hateful behavior. People who seemed to lack any sense of empathy."

"Oh, he knew what he was doing, the way he'd cut up those Bibles."

It was pointless. Despite her issues with Greg Peifer, Joyce was the least critical human being I'd ever known, especially when it came to her sons. She always saw the best in them, and when that was impossible, called upon her titanic powers of denial. All that was left was the ultimate question, the one I had been curious about my entire life: Was she sorry she never had a girl?

"No, never," she replied without hesitation. "With girls, you worry all the time. Boys are easier."

Good Christ. *Easier?*

"Can you imagine having a teenage daughter and she comes home pregnant?"

Yes! By one of your awful sons!

"Poor Linda Kaufman, just when she can finally relax,

she's raising Amy's two kids. No, I'll take boys any day. They're more manageable."

CRACK! CRACK! CRACK!

My daughter was born at nearly the stroke of midnight during an unseasonably warm November. After double-checking her vagina a few times, I became euphoric, feeling as though I, too, had just emerged from the birth canal. Perspective and priorities came into sharp focus, and I was infused with an overwhelming sensation of love and gratitude. Is this what people experience when they're baptized, I wondered? But the smell of a new car wears off quickly, and as the nurse administered drops to the baby's eyes, I was already having thoughts of a runaway meth-addicted wild child petitioning SUVs on Las Vegas Boulevard. Was my mother right? Were boys easier?

The lights in the birthing room suddenly went out, leaving only a dull yellow bulb that illuminated my daughter.

The infant lifted its head (a remarkable feat for a newborn) and bore into me with cloudy but commanding eyes still oozing silver nitrate.

"Get some help, motherfucker," she rasped.

"I will, darling," I replied. "I'll do it for you."

She managed a half-assed thumbs-up and the lights returned.

I followed through on my promise, but had a few ground rules going in. I made it clear to the therapist that things like "working on forgiveness"—specifically regarding my brothers— were off the table; he was welcome to "witch me" any way that moved him, but I wasn't willing to delve into the past or hawk up bad memories. We'd have to figure it out. Cartoon dollar signs appeared in his eyes. Then he gave me a prescription for some pills that dulled my ability to think, kept me drowsy, and took the wind out of my penis. I saw the hand of God in every capsule.

When Sadie was about three, we traveled to Harrisburg to visit my parents, now living in a small home not far from the old one. During a lull, I took her on a drive to show her where I grew up. Little of it remained. By now the brothers were scattered across North America, in New York, Kansas, California, Arizona, and Florida. A few of us kept in touch, while some hadn't spoken to others in years. The house itself was gone, along with the street, demolished and plowed under to make room for strip malls and townhomes. The gurgling blister of my childhood had crusted over and was now a Walgreens. Sadie seemed confused.

"You lived in a store?" she remarked.

"No, sweetie, my house used to be where the store is."

"But what happened to it?"

"They knocked it down."

"Did you cry?"

I walked her through the aisles, trying to orient myself and figure out the house's former footprint, eventually finding a section that approximated where my bedroom once existed. And just like that, there we were: father and daughter, standing in my old room, gazing at the enema kits. Like an old soldier returning to Normandy, I tried to conjure up memories and emotions, but the only thing I felt was the small sticky hand holding on to mine.

Blue Yodel No. 13

Emerging from the swamps of Cogdell, Georgia, Gina Erdmann migrated north to Pennsylvania with her mother, Janice,
when she was ten. There was a husband at some point—Gina's
father—who'd fallen by the wayside when she was an infant;
and later, a second husband, who vaporized after some money
from a construction accident came his way. For a time they
lived with Janice's mother in Enola, Pennsylvania, but eventually moved into a little brick house one neighborhood over
from mine, where the yards were a little shabbier and dogs ran
around with plastic doll arms in their mouths. By the time
Gina was sixteen, it was common knowledge that she was an

easy lay, and for me, that was really the only biographical information of any importance.

I was fifteen at the time and still hadn't "done it" yet, and like most boys that age, the fevered urge for sex created a kind of nuclear fission in my body so powerful that if dropped from an F-16, I was capable of blowing up a city the size of Roanoke, Virginia. In fact, I had barely noticed Gina Erdmann in the classrooms and hallways of our high school. My interest in her only surfaced as word started getting around that she liked to smoke pot and fuck. It was the second part that got my attention. Soon, compelling terms like "freak" and "nymphomaniac" were bandied about, bringing the hype to a rolling boil until I could no longer ignore it. This was the sort of girl I needed in my life.

Gina was no great beauty, but then neither was I. She was gangly, wore heaps of raccoon mascara, and had crayon-yellow hair that hung from her head like overcooked spaghettini. The skunky black stripe down the middle of her scalp brought to mind a trail of ants walking through a puddle of Cheez Whiz. A judgmental type might describe her as "cheap looking." Still, her face wasn't bad exactly, but she did have quite a honker. From certain angles, she was a dead ringer for Gandy Goose, a cartoon character I enjoyed as a child but never fantasized about banging. Her best features were a slight Southern accent, which she tried to hide, and a smart-ass insolence that often got her into trouble. She was suspended once for calling Miss Gladfelter a dyke bitch and another time for telling Mr. Lutz to suck her balls. This was a feisty, angry girl—something I found both horrifying and thrilling. Whether she ever noticed me, I had no idea. If she was attracted to scrawny boys with skin the color of Wonder Bread and coal-black Little Orphan Annie curls, she never let on. Ultimately, though, it was beside the point. This was simply about plying her with marijuana as a prologue to sex, an activity she so ravenously enjoyed. The tricky part would be getting to know her better, since a single word had never passed between us.

This proved to be an easy task. Our first formal introduction was made in the woodsy area behind the Gulf station across from the high school: a popular setting where kids hung out, smoked cigarettes, and—if you were a dipshit like Henry Daubert—did their homework. It was there that I casually engaged the gang in a conversation about what a dyke bitch Miss Gladfelter was. Gina immediately agreed. The ice had been broken. Somehow I made a seamless transition to "Boy, do I love pot. In fact, I'm going to be buying some really good pot after school this Friday." Gina laughingly said, "Don't forget about me when you get that shit." I told her she was welcome to come along if she'd like. "Sure," she replied.

Gee whiz! I thought. *I'm gonna get laid!*

Now it was just about a few minor details. The good news

was I really did know a pot dealer—Jeff Glogower, who was a friend of my brother Jack. Unfortunately, he lived way out in Markelsville. But maybe the long drive would be a nice opportunity for Gina and me to get to know each other better (heh-heh). From my understanding, those nymphos got all worked up when they were in a state of anticipation. Yes, it was all falling into place . . . except the part where I was only fifteen and didn't have a license and had to sneak my mom's car out. It wasn't as if I hadn't slipped the old lady's Cutlass out plenty of times before, but it was always late at night. The daylight logistics would be a bit of a sticky wicket.

I needn't have worried. It turned out that Joyce and a few of her friends were going on a bus trip to Philly that Friday to see a taping of *The Mike Douglas Show*. The car would be at my complete disposal. Apparently Mike and the gods had deemed I should get my ashes hauled.

I arrived home immediately after school on Friday, ate a bowl of Honeycombs for stamina, and grabbed the keys. I pulled up to Gina's house at the predetermined hour of three o'clock. Everything was calculated down to the minute. The itinerary went something like this:

Twenty-five minutes to get to Glogower's place and buy the pot.

Twenty-five minutes to return to Gina's house and start smoking the pot. (Her mother would be at work by then.)

Twenty minutes of pot smoking and chitchat, followed by . . .

Making out—3–5 minutes. Followed by . . .

Fucking—30 minutes.

Short breather—5 minutes. Then . . .

Thirty more minutes of fucking.

Total approximate time with a little padding: 2 hours and 30 minutes. I'd easily make it home by six, and my mother wasn't due back from Philadelphia until seven. Pretty good for a guy who was flunking pre-algebra.

The Cutlass idled for nearly ten minutes in front of Gina's house, but no sign of her. Mindful of the timetable and getting hornier by the second, I killed the engine and knocked on the front door. Her mother, Janice, answered, cigarette dangling from her lips and wearing a Baskin-Robbins uniform that had a coffee stain on the right boob (which also made me horny). She looked like a cross between Loni Anderson and Barry Manilow, and I instantly saw where Gina inherited her nose.

"Look, I paid the goddamn thing," she informed me in an accent more prominent than her daughter's. "I told that to the last runt they sent over."

After it was clarified that I didn't work for the newspaper and her subscription would continue uninterrupted, I explained I was there to pick up Gina. "Gina?" she retorted with a hoot. "You mean that dead dog back in the bedroom? She's out like a light."

I sat in a small area off the kitchen, gazing at my reflection in the blank screen of a RCA Colortrak. On top of the TV was a framed picture of Gina from elementary school. She looked like an otter with glasses. A couple of decorative plates depicting bullfighters hung from the wall, and the breakfront appeared to be a storage nook for cat food and cleaning supplies. I could hear Mrs. Erdmann and Gina yelling at each other from the bedroom.

"I said I'm getting up!" Gina screeched. "Get the fuck out of my room!"

"Is that my cigarette lighter?" her mother demanded.

"No!"

"I buy 'em and you lose 'em."

"I didn't touch your fucking lighters! I have my own lighter!"

"I know that every time I see the burnt shower curtain."

"It exploded!"

"Who smokes in the shower anyway?"

"It exploded!"

"Let's get Cricket on the phone. I've bought hundreds of those lighters, they never blew up on me."

"Mommy! Get the fuck out of my room!"

Moments later, mother and daughter were sitting across

from me in the courting parlor, smoking like pros. They had calmed down somewhat, evidently sharing the one pastime they enjoyed as a family. Gina's eyes were slits. She was guzzling coffee and told me to give her a few minutes to wake up. Mrs. Erdmann told her if she got sleep at *night*, when *normal* people sleep, she wouldn't be tired all day.

"Crawl out of my ass, Janice!" Gina replied, as she tore open a pack of mini-donuts with her teeth, creating a mushroom cloud of powdered sugar.

Her mother chuckled and playfully threw a pillow at her. Gina deflected it with a dirty foot.

"Jesus, it's like living with a child," Gina said as she stubbed out her Kool 100 and stuffed a donut in her mouth.

There was a lull in the conversation. Mrs. Erdmann glanced over and caught me staring at the stain on her uniform. She smiled.

"Look at those long curls, Gina," she said, pointing her cigarette at me. "Just like Bernadette Peters. I'd pay a million dollars for curls like that."

Gina let out a frustrated grunt. "Come on, Resnick, let's go."

She kissed her mother goodbye and told her we were going to Sears to buy notebooks.

My entire body was quaking as we walked toward the door. This was no longer a fantasy. The plan was in motion and I was going to have sex with this girl! Could I even make it to Jeff Glogower's and back? Was the pot really necessary? I was ready right *now*, willing to take on all comers: Gina, her mother—*gulp*—both at the same time?

That's when it caught my eye: the box in the corner of the den. The one containing a stack of old records—78s. I slammed on the brakes.

"Are those your records?" I asked Mrs. Erdmann.

"Oh, God, no. They're my mom's," she replied. "I was over there, clearing out some of her junk. I got a bunch of garbage I'm taking over to the auction next Wednesday."

Gina was halfway out the door, but I was hovering over the box. Right away I saw a Victor scroll label on the top of the stack. I knelt down and my eyes focused. Was I really seeing it? Jimmie Rodgers's "Gambling Polka Dot Blues"? Underneath were two more Jimmie Rodgers sides in VG+ condition. I was staggered.

"Your mother listens to Jimmie Rodgers?" I gasped.

"Ha-ha, oh, yeah. She's a real corncob. Came up here from deep Georgia. She likes those old fiddle tunes and the rest. You listen to that stuff? Take 'em if you like."

My love for old music began when I was a kid. It started with early jazz, which I just knew as cartoon music—the stuff that played while assorted animals that had no business being together on the same continent, let alone in the same luncheonette, danced around and washed dishes. There was something about that krazy-syncopated rhythm that hit my brain just right and made me happy. And trust me, I was never happy. Much later, when I began searching it out, I learned that the sound I loved so much was recorded primarily between 1926 and 1933—before the first nauseating strains of swing music crept in and fucked up everything that was authentic and beautiful.

By thirteen I'd started scouring flea markets, junk shops, yard sales—anywhere that might have these hard-to-find records I was looking for. I got to know a few old-timers and collectors who turned me on to early blues, country, and string bands—all the great stuff. While my contemporaries gathered after school to socialize, smoke weed, and listen to Pink Floyd, I'd rush home, lock myself in my room, and blast my near-mint-condition copy of "Hatchet Head Blues" by the Old Southern Jug Band (which, as any asshole knows, is a nom de guerre for Clifford Hayes's Dixieland Jug Blowers).

There were several blues and hillbilly singers whose songs of grief, dread, and futility spoke to me. These were feelings I'd known since the first day of kindergarten. But Jimmie Rodgers held a special place in my heart. He had the ability to sing about life's miseries with an air of jubilance, all in a warm, reedy voice that seemed to imply, Don't worry, partner, you'll get through it. Just the sound of his yodel was an elixir for my anxious mind. (That is, until antidepressants came along, which were more effective but less poetic.)

To Gina's annoyance, I was now sitting on the floor, digging through the stack of records. Fiddlin' John Carson! The Blue Sky Boys! Uncle Dave Macon! (And not just any Uncle Dave Macon—the incomparable "Rabbit in the Pea Patch.") I had never come across this many great records in one place. Then Mrs. Erdmann said something that made me almost pass out.

"Yeah, Mom's even got a record at home with Jimmie Rodgers's picture right on it."

I took a deep breath. *Please tell me I heard what I thought I just heard.*

"You mean an old record like one of these?" I asked, voice trembling.

"Uh-huh. He's right on there, holding his guitar and whatnot."

The 78s I had found at the Erdmann house were already astounding by any standard, but what this woman was describing, what she was so casually *tossing out* like an empty pack of Merit 100's, could be only one thing: the legendary Jimmie Rodgers picture disc.

Without any prior history of epilepsy, I nearly swallowed my tongue.

But before I continue, A Brief Symposium on the Above Topic (the record, not epilepsy):

Shortly after his death in 1933, RCA Victor pressed a limited number of copies of one of Jimmie Rodgers's last recordings, the prophetic "Cowhand's Last Ride." A photograph of the great "Singing Brakeman" was emblazoned on the A side of the disc, making it an instant collector's item (an idiotic term that didn't exist in 1933, when food was the prize collectible). To this day, RCA Victor 18-6000 remains one of the rarest and most sought-after records in country music history.

Luck was not something I was accustomed to, but sometimes life boils down to one good lead. As I gently put the box of 78s into the back of the car, I felt like I had the world by the balls. My carefully planned itinerary would have to be revised; getting that record was now my top priority. *Then* would come the pot, *then* would come the fucking. What a day. Perhaps the mythic hellhounds were no longer on my trail.

This new mission had to be handled cautiously. I needed Gina's cooperation, but it was becoming increasingly clear that she was a difficult girl, if not completely nuts. We were only on the road a few minutes when I realized we had virtually nothing to talk about and nothing in common. She produced a bag of pizza-flavored Goldfish crackers from her denim purse and devoured them as if she'd just been pulled aboard a Russian trawler after six days at sea clinging to a deck chair. Soon the entire car smelled like vomit. It was time to make my move.

"Hey, would you mind if we stopped by your grandmother's real quick?"

"*What?*" she responded in a tone that suggested I was speaking another language.

"Just that old record she has. The one your mom was telling me about."

"What the fuck are you talking about?"

"The Jimmie Rodgers record. You know, the one with the picture on—"

"Hey, does your guy have speed?"

This was obviously going to be a chore.

"I know he has pot. I didn't ask about speed."

She burned a Kool and flicked ashes on my mother's carpet. A mile later, I approached the subject again.

"So, where does your grandma live, anyway?"

"*What?*"

"I mean, does she live around here? In the general vicinity?"

"She's over in Camelot Village. Who gives a shit? Fuck! I hate when I get gunk in my eye!"

She dug a knuckle into her eye socket. A half mile later . . .

"So, did you wanna shoot over there real quick? Camelot Village?"

"Why the fuck would I want to go to my grandmother's? What's wrong with you, Resnick?"

Gina downed the last bit of Goldfish crumbs, shaking them directly into her mouth. I glanced over as she licked each of her greasy yellow fingers in a manner that was not particularly erotic. Then she balled up the bag and flung it in the backseat.

"Why do my fucking toes always itch?" she said, kicking off a clog.

My mother had returned home from Philadelphia earlier than expected and was in a crabby mood. *The Mike Douglas Show* had been a bust—she and her friends were expecting to see Leslie Uggams but, due to a scheduling change, got Buddy Rich. "What an obnoxious idiot! He pounds on those drums like a baboon!" According to my brother Jack, she immediately noticed the Cutlass was gone and hit the roof. Later, I learned, he not only ratted me out but also stirred the pot by suggesting, "If he gets in an accident and kills someone, we'll end up living under a bridge." Joyce stormed outside and stood in the driveway, hands on hips, waiting for my return. Jack joined her and was nice enough to mention that the car was low on oil.

If only she knew her Cutlass was well beyond the township border, headed toward that dreamy, not-so-faraway land called Perry County, where a Mr. Jeff Glogower was expecting me—shirtless, grandly reposed on a cherry-colored velour sofa, smoking a joint and caressing a Honduran milk snake that dozed in his lap.

My efforts to convince Gina that it would be "fun" to stop by her grandmother's had failed. She displayed little interest in my lecture on Jimmie Rodgers and his influence on American music and showed a blatant lack of fascination when I discussed his brief stint running a transfer car for the old M&O line out of Okolona, Mississippi. I can now conclusively state, so that future generations of young men might learn, that a protracted dialogue relating to the famed Singing Brakeman is not the way into a girl's pants.

I decided to back off for the time being. If I had any hopes of getting my hands on that record, I'd have to follow through on my promise and buy her some dope. After that, perhaps, she would have the common courtesy to think about *my* needs. In the meantime, little distractions like her announcement that she needed to "buy cigarettes and take a crap" ate into both the timetable and my libido.

We crossed over into Perry County, and I was instantly reminded of the discomfort I always felt when entering the region. Perry County was boisterous no-muffler territory, a land of proud, sun-crowned Aryans who enjoyed the great outdoors in all its savage glory. Indeed, even indoors felt like outdoors here, where the art of taxidermy was plentiful and existed on its lowest rung. In a typical living room, one might find the head of a spectacular white-tailed buck possessing the teeth of a cartoon Chinaman, or a skunk with saucer eyes arched in some hypermobilic position that nature, on its cruelest day, never intended. Perry County was also home to an overromanticized eatery that drew gastronomes from as far away as Grantville and Hummelstown. Gina suddenly let out a shriek: "Resnick, stop! The Red Rabbit!"

Within moments I found myself parked at the old carhop joint, watching Gina tear into a bacon cheeseburger and french fries with extra "bunny dust." The legendary bunny dust, one of Red Rabbit's most popular rabbit-themed condiments, was, as far as I could tell, that exotic spice commonly known as pepper. The car, already funky from cigarettes, Goldfish crackers, and Charlie perfume, now smelled like a rendering plant. Mindful of the time, I urged Gina along, but she was battling a piece of gristle wedged between two back molars. Her opponent was no match, however, and was finally expelled through the passenger window. As we departed, her stumpy fingers rooted through my mom's glove compartment, searching for a toothpick. She settled for the registration card and my stomach wept.

I might have been more anxious had I known my mother, cheered on by my brother Jack, was on the phone with the police, ordering them to track me down and haul me in. The township cops were always bored and itching for some action. Once they got the call, their flattops were at full bristle, and all other crime—like kids popping wheelies in the library parking lot—would have to wait. Armed with fresh Slurpees in their cup holders, the officers decamped, and the manhunt for Bonnie and Clyde began.

Jeff Glogower's home was tucked away at the end of a long narrow path where wild vegetation reached out spastically, scraping the side of the car, which squealed as if being gutted. Soon the house sprouted from the earth, tall, narrow, and unfinished: a wood-framed vertical shoebox with high slender windows and a flat roof (pronounced "ruff" in this fiefdom). Architecturally, it looked like a lunatic's take on early-1960s modern. (Though the year was 1978, the seventies would not officially arrive in Perry County for at least two more decades, so one could argue it was downright futuristic.) Jeff was constructing his new residence with the help of a few other Glogowers—big-bearded cousins who roamed around like apes in a private jungle.

Our little stop-off at the Red Rabbit had wasted valuable time. I instructed Gina to sit tight while I fetched the weed, but she balked, complaining of a "shit fly" in the car that kept landing on her tit. It was a statement that left me with little negotiating power.

Jeff Glogower opened the door, barely acknowledging us

as we entered. He was in mid-conversation with one of his cousins, who held up two linoleum floor tiles. Aesthetic merits were briefly debated before Jeff decisively tapped an injured black fingernail on his preference, stating, "That's the cocksucker." "Cocksucker" was a popular word among Glogowers. It was used as a curse ("That cocksucker owes me money"), a term of endearment ("Five years old and the little cocksucker taught himself to swim"), and a synonym for anything from a pipe wrench to an Oreo ("Hand me that cocksucker" and "Damn, these cocksuckers are good," respectively).

The living room, like the rest of house, was still rough, littered with power tools and candy wrappers. Jeff collapsed on the sofa and lit a joint, appearing in no particular hurry to conduct business. Tall and barrel-chested, he dangled his legs off the arm of the couch as he absentmindedly wobbled a floor lamp between his toes. With his long, sweaty blond hair falling over one eye, he looked like a disturbing blend of Teddy Roosevelt and Veronica Lake. Gina and I took the only two chairs, which were upholstered in some sort of mystery fabric that was coarse and nubby; it was like sitting on a dog covered in oak burrs. Jeff suddenly sat up, as if forgetting something, and reached for a snake that was nesting on an orange crate. He laid it on his bare stomach and said, "This dude's my belly warmer." Gina laughed hysterically. Her level of amusement was lost on me.

"Ain't seen you in a while, Resnick," Jeff remarked. "What's your brother up to?"

"Nothing."

"You know he's fucking crazy, right?"

"Yeah."

Gina emitted a scream that almost propelled me off the dog-chair. A tegu lizard with a large cyst on its tail had entered the room, tongue flickering, and meandered toward a pan of kitty litter. Jeff threw a motorcycle magazine at it.

"Get the fuck out of there, bitch!"

He shook his head in annoyance. "Motherfucker always wants to lay in the shitbox."

"What's that thing on his tail?" Gina asked.

"Just got himself a booger. 'Bout ten I'll give him a calcium pill."

"Awwww," she cooed as she walked over and knelt by the lizard. "Can I hold him or will he bite me?"

"Nah, he don't bite. But he might piss on you."

Gina picked up the tegu like it was an infant she'd found on her doorstep. Settling back in her chair, she cradled it, bringing to mind the iconic image of Madonna and Child. I felt a little out of place, being the only person in the room without a reptile resting on his body. Jeff lit a fresh joint and passed it my way. "You wanna try something special? This shit came from the Amazon." Geography aside, the notion of "special pot" meant very little to me. I was wound so tight, nothing short of anesthesia could get me to relax. Still, in the interest of moving things along, I took a hit and passed it to Gina. She gestured for me to put the joint between her lips so as not to startle the scaly infant she rocked in the crook of her arm. Oddly, the whole combo turned me on. "Who wants to see a baby red-tailed boa?" Jeff suddenly asked with great enthusiasm. Gina frantically waved her hand in the air. I tried to remind her of the time, but she was already trailing him up the temporary plywood stair boards.

I waited in the bristly chair, holding the joint, worried that a stray ember might fall on the petroleum-based fabric and blow the house up. I smoked it down for lack of anything better to do and dropped the roach in a half-empty can of Schaefer. Through the tall, skinny windows, I caught a glimpse of a stray Glogower urinating on what appeared to be a dead beehive.

The first indication that something was off was when I spotted the tegu lizard slowly ambling its way downstairs, trailed by the apple-sized cyst that landed on each step with a thump. I abruptly heard Gina cry out, and imagined a Gaboon viper dangling from her arm by its fangs. Heading for the stairs, I heard another scream, but quickly realized it was not the sound of distress. Far from it. Gina and Jeff Glogower were fucking.

I stopped and sat down on one of the step boards for a little think, but my mind was a mess. Soon, though, I began to feel calm, as the voice of Jimmie Rodgers echoed in my head, singing "I'm Sorry We Met." Through the window I swore I saw an old freight train disappear through the pine trees. Wow, listen to that whistle! But it wasn't a whistle; it was Gina, still howling from upstairs. She did not emit the garden-variety noises of lovemaking; beyond the occasional "Yes!" "Right there!" and "Don't stop!" it sounded more like someone stabbing a wolf pup.

I needed more marijuana.

Then the front door kicked open and one of Jeff's cousins entered holding a paving stone, which he dropped on a floor tarp, sending a cloud of dust in the air. "Tell him we're going with this cocksucker." I nodded in approval and he departed. A few more yelps bounced off the drywall, and Jeff's winded voice called out from upstairs, "Is that my Belgium block?"

The drive out of Perry County was awkward. I gave Gina the silent treatment, which had little effect since she was sleeping. Certainly she must have known what my intentions were that afternoon. Wasn't it abundantly clear? I had a very detailed plan! Days in the making! Somehow, Jeff Glogower achieved the same objective with less effort than it takes to feed a mouse to a Malayan horned frog.

But it was all bunny dust under the bridge now: I had lost

interest in having sex with Gina Erdmann. Beyond my bruised feelings, she was a walking fuck-you to rudimentary hygiene. The whole escapade had been a bust, my carefully planned timeline shot. And what about that Amazonian reefer—was it possibly having an effect on me? Could just a few puffs make my head feel like a balloon slowly untethering from a fence post?

I heard the unexpected sound of Gina's voice.

"You ever been in a car wreck, Resnick?" she asked through an extended yawn.

"No," I replied curtly. "Have you ever been in a car wreck?"

"Once. A couple of years ago."

She lifted her bangs to reveal a long scar under the hairline.

"What happened?"

"I don't remember. Scott Yoder was driving. You know him?"

"I've seen him."

"Yah, well, he's a fat queer."

She lit a cigarette.

"But you don't know when you're in a car wreck. It's fucking weird. You just touch your head and it's all wet and you're laying in some lady's yard with bloody towels all over the place."

Somewhere in the distance, I heard the train whistle again, and I started to perspire. Was I dead? Had I just been killed in a car crash? I vaguely remembered smoking poison. What the hell was she talking about? This fucking chick was a phantom! Did I die because of this bitch?

Gina belched, bringing me slightly back to earth.

"So, you wanna go get your record?" she asked.

I was in love with her.

Something like civilization returned as we arrived back in Susquehanna Township and passed through two fake watch-towers that marked the entrance to Camelot Village. Gina's grandmother lived on King Arthur's Court, just south of Sir Lancelot Circle. My father's voice came to me with familiar words from the past: "Whoever came up with that place is a first-class asshole."

Gina pounded several times on her grandmother's front door, rattling a panel of faux stained glass that depicted the image of a koala bear flying a kite. "Blinker!" she called out several times. "Blinker, open the goddamn door!" I don't know why she called her grandmother "Blinker." I just assumed it was an affectionate nickname for someone with age-related eye disease. An old coot dragging a garden hose from the garage next door confirmed what I was already fearing: "If you're looking for Blinker, she just got the bus."

"Fuck!" I blurted out, kicking the peat moss.

"That won't turn the bus around, boy," he chastised.

Gina grabbed my arm and led me around the building where she proceeded to pry open a window. I didn't like where this was going. Sensing my trepidation, she assured me: "Don't worry. I steal her shit all the time. She's fucking retarded."

That worked for me. I had brothers who'd done worse. Besides, it was getting late, and in truth, I was only rescuing something that was meant to be mine. The grandmother couldn't possibly understand Jimmie Rodgers the way I did. How could she?

I hoisted Gina up and through the window and ran around to the front door. Luckily, the coot was gone. The koala swung open. It had been a long slog, but I was in.

The blinds were drawn and the apartment was dark. Somewhere a clock was ticking. My head began to thud. "Hurry! Look for the fucking thing!" Gina hissed. I lurched from room to room, searching. My Red Wing boots left imprints on the carpet. Evidence! I rifled through cabinets, closets, and dresser drawers, seeing things I had no business seeing. What was I doing here? Somewhere I heard the sound of glass rattling. Gina was loading a shopping bag with scotch and other prizes. I staggered into the living room and ripped the guts out of a pine hutch. A moment of sunlight bathed the stained glass and a strange rainbow appeared on the wall. It was in the shape of a grizzly bear killing an old lady while flying a kite. Was someone spraying water somewhere?. The coot! He's on to us! No, it was just Gina taking a leak. Oh, that infernal ticking! It trailed me everywhere, getting deeper, louder! A silhouette of Gina clutching a shower radio skittered by in the hallway. I called out to her. She paused as a stab of light hit her eye. That eye! That red reptilian eye! I stumbled backward toward the kitchen as if I were being pulled. Throbbing drums! Jungle drums! Beating inside my very skull! I'm coming, Jimmie! Lead me! I fell into the tight, crooked room where a steady drip banged on aluminum. A box of Kellogg's All-Bran stood on the counter like a sentry. The ticking, the dripping, the drums, everything became more rapid, more fevered. "Yes, Jimmie, yes! Don't stop! Right there!" The empty kettle suddenly whistled as it pulled into the station. My eyes followed the steam as it rose higher and higher, forming a great cloud in Blinker's kitchen. Then, all at once, it dissipated. And I could see.

Hanging on the wall, right above the sink, where Gina Erdmann's grandmother washed her dishes, was the Jimmie Rodgers picture record. It had been fashioned into a clock. A clock with imitation gold hands and a fake pendulum that hung lamely like the tail of a dead stingray. It was hideous. It was blasphemous.

I reached up and gently freed it from the nail. Somewhere I heard a sigh. It was Gina, standing behind me.

"*That's* what you wanted? A fucking clock? God, that's ugly."

I hushed her and somberly placed it on the kitchen table to begin the autopsy. I turned it over to inspect the B side of the clock. Back in its halcyon days, when it was still a record, I would have seen the title "Blue Yodel No. 12" (aka "Barefoot Blues"), but it was all gone, painted over for some inexplicable reason with mustard-colored paint. The center hole had been clumsily enlarged to make room for the quartz mechanism that was affixed with black electrical tape and contained two C batteries. I flipped it back over and gazed at the face of Jimmie Rodgers, old pal of my heart, smiling at me through the cracked laminate.

Then, I noticed the time.

We exited fast, Gina with a bag of liquor and her grandmother's wedding ring, and me with the clock—which I intended to bury. The apartment door slammed shut just as the corner of my eye caught sight of my mother. The remainder of the eye found the cop, the coot, and my brother Jack's shit-eating grin.

I sat alone in the backseat of the Cutlass, no longer captain of my vessel. The clock and the box of records from

Gina's mom had been confiscated. I would never see them again. Through the windshield I watched as the officer spoke to my mother, occasionally using a dramatic hand gesture. She was comforted by my brother, who had his arm around her, shaking his head in mock disbelief. What a fuckwad. Gina, meanwhile, sat defiantly in the back of the police cruiser. When the cop had asked her where her mother could be reached, she replied, "Up my ass."

My mom stewed silently for the first thirty seconds of the ride home and then erupted.

"Do you know what that cop told me? He said that girl's run away from home three times! The last time with a thirty-two-year-old man!"

Jack chimed in from the passenger seat. "What normal person would be involved with a girl like *that*? She's not even pretty."

"She comes from a bad home," my mom continued. "She's been in trouble with drugs and everything else."

"I just hope she doesn't rob *us* now," Jack added with concern.

"I don't want you anywhere near her again! And you can forget about using my car—*ever*! I don't care if you're sixteen or sixty!"

"Actually, I don't know if he'll even be able to *get* a

license now," Jack pointed out. "They'll probably make him wait until he's twenty-one."

"Good!"

"My friend's dad is a Lower Paxton cop. I'll ask him."

"Shut the fuck up, Jack!" I snapped.

My mother started to tear up.

"First Buddy Rich, and now this."

Well, it's all shit from here, I thought. *And Merv's not even home yet.*

The hellhounds had not lost my scent. Nor would they ever. I knew they would shadow me all the way to the grave. (The irony is, I like dogs.) The road ahead looked long and dreary. I was only fifteen.

Yet just moments before, as my mother drove out of Camelot Village, we passed the patrol car in the parking lot. Gina was in the backseat. She looked bored. We caught sight of each other and she waved to me, bouncing up and down with an excited grin that seemed to say "We did it!" What we did exactly was unclear to me, but it was certainly something. She was a special one, Gina Erdmann. Had Jimmie Rodgers met her, he might've written a song about her. And then hopped a train to the next town.

The Strand Bag

Although friends, family, and casual acquaintances might violently disagree, I consider myself a simple man with simple needs. Like the gentle field cow that requires little more than to be grazed and watered, I'm the very definition of "easy keeper."

Per my modest routine each morning, I carry a legal pad, a blue retractable pen, and a piece of fruit twelve blocks to the small studio apartment I rent as an office. Throughout the years I've transported these items in a variety of plastic shopping bags: Fairway, Gap, CVS, Saigon Grill—they've all had their turn and they've all come up short. For a brief period there was even a very nice Tumi messenger tote that my wife bought me one Christmas—unfortunately, I was daunted by all the zippers and compartments and disliked the sensation of a strap on my shoulder, which, quite honestly, made me feel like a drag queen. But somewhere along the line, in this blur of bags, I became monogamous with "the one." We've all been there, right?

The Strand Book Store on lower Broadway is one of New York City's great marvels, boasting 18 MILES OF BOOKS. Never mind that you'll want to blow your brains out after ten minutes because there are *too many fucking books*, simply jostle and elbow your way through the three congested sales floors and, in time, you'll exit with some reasonably priced treasure like *Vintage Cracker Jack Toys and Premiums, 1912–1940* (seconds of pleasure) or an insightfully balanced volume probing the mind-set of ordinary Germans during World War II (yeah, right, they were brainwashed—*please*). In my several yearly visits to the Strand, I have, books aside, always been assured to walk out with something I've considered very special: a superbly designed shopping bag that feels so good in my hand that it elevates my dopamine levels and helps bring my skeletal frame into proper alignment.

Allow me to continue.

While I wouldn't characterize my fondness for the bag as obsessive, a few particulars are worth noting. Made of luxurious two-ply, wrinkle-resistant plastic, the cheerful red-and-yellow Strand bag measures thirteen inches wide by seventeen inches tall. Comfortable oval-shaped handle openings are perfectly positioned approximately an inch and a half below the top lip. These openings are reinforced and made even more pleasing by a bordering strip of clear plastic on the inner side. The base of the bag has been blessed with a tight inward pleat that prevents slackness and eliminates the dreaded "puffing out" effect so common with its lesser colleagues. Contents remain snug, upright, and balanced. (For all you Freudists enjoying a cheap titter, grow up.)

To carry this little wonder around is one of life's simple joys—a rare example of perfection in a woefully imperfect world.

The trouble began when I happened upon an old photograph of myself tentatively feeding a mentally ill water frog. The frog, purchased from a mail-order company in Loxley, Alabama, was prone to psychotic episodes that sent it zipping full-speed through the algae before it smashed its face into the side of the tank and vomited. I think it was also blind. In the picture, the Strand bag can be seen resting on a chair in the background, safely set away from the splash of amphibian puke-water.

As I studied the image, I crunched the numbers: The

frog was purchased for my daughter's seventh birthday and only lived twenty-six days (which I'm sure it considered twenty-six days too long). If the bag went back as far as the frog, that meant I'd been carrying it or one of its identical siblings around for almost a decade. A question arose inside me faster than a country songwriter jots down "gravel road" on a lyric sheet: *Am I out of my mind?*

The easy answer, of course, was "yes." But was I *that* kind of crazy? When I left the apartment in the morning, did the regulars along West End Avenue think of me as the "Strand Bag Guy"? I was particularly concerned about a group of teenagers I often passed as they waited for the school bus. Was my memory playing tricks on me, or had I sometimes heard laughter as I walked by? And why was I suddenly recalling phrases like "Nice bag, Porky"?

I made a few inquiries to a short list of people whose opinions I trusted, starting with my wife. "Hey, you know how I carry that Strand bag around every day? Is that a little . . . funny?" Her *I dunno* shrug was as big and phony as Jethro's twin sister Jethrine in *The Beverly Hillbillies* (Google it at your own risk), and her follow-up was even more telling: "What happened to that nice Tumi messenger tote I bought you for Christmas?" My friend Julie responded with a similar non-answer answer: "You should check out J.Crew. They have some really nice backpacks." (Then shot me an email with a link to amplify her point.) And Jill, a close colleague with a certain obnoxious candor, merely stated, "You look insane."

I was a little annoyed that people close to me had a negative view of the bag yet had said nothing all the years I'd been carrying it around. Was Lorrie biting her lip as I left the apartment each morning, only to burst out laughing when the door closed? Did she watch me from the tenth-floor window as I walked down the street, thinking, *No wonder I'm banging the guy I met at the dog run?*

I decided to seek out a more reliable opinion. As luck would have it, I knew a mental health practitioner who I habitually bumped into twice a week for forty-five minutes. Certainly he'd seen the bag in my possession and never commented.

I sat down with him and laid it out: I don't suffer from OCD, I'm not making an environmental statement about reusing stuff, nor am I trying to cultivate the image of a cool, eccentric writer who, à la Tom Wolfe and his white suit, is never seen without a plastic shopping bag. Can't a man just ferry his possessions from place to place in the repository of his choice? Must we be judged by even our most benign habits and routines?

The doctor sat in thoughtful silence, struggling to stay awake. Finally, he replied, "Whatever happened to that nice messenger bag your wife bought you for Christmas?"

Another wiseass.

Then came the capper—he challenged me to throw the bag away in his presence. "Just, as, well, sort of an experiment." "But what about all my stuff?" I protested. "How am I gonna lug around a pen, a notepad, and a Ziploc full of blueberries? Am I supposed to shove 'em up my ass?" The "genius" had no comeback.

I stormed out of his office with the bag and its contents intact. Three blocks later I concluded he was 100 percent right and I belonged in an institution. Without further delay, I removed the pad, pen, and blueberries and tossed the bag into a garbage can. Fuck it.

I continued down the sidewalk, making it a full ten steps before my belongings got the best of me. I dropped the pen and almost blew my back out saving the blueberries. The legal pad ended up in a puddle, where drowned cigarette butts clung to it like leeches. I huffed back to the trash can, furious that I'd been manipulated into making such a rash decision, arriving just in time to see a guy using my bag to pick up some dog shit. (The irony of shit inside the very bag that normally contained my writing somehow escaped me at the time; the shrink made a point of hammering it home a few sessions later.)

I refused to make a big deal over the fact that I was on the No. 3 train within minutes, headed downtown to the Strand.

Or that my mouth felt abnormally dry and I was unconsciously scratching my neck, leaving long red scrape marks. I simply needed a new bag, and this was no time to read into things. As it was, I was dropping blueberries all over the train and not a single passenger offered to help gather them.

The store was typically packed when I arrived. The Strand is often less about shopping and more about finding an air pocket. Thankfully, I just needed to grab a quick book so I could get what I really came for. But for the first time in fifteen years and hundreds of visits, I could find nothing of interest. I must have combed through at least five of the 18 Miles of Books, checking all my usual haunts. There was nothing new or fun on the Nazi table, the photography section was clogged with oversize volumes depicting civil unrest in the sixties, and no matter where I looked, I came upon towering stacks of *A Tree Grows in Brooklyn*. Ultimately, I settled on a slender, inexpensive Beat poet anthology, which had been misplaced on the Lesbian Erotica shelf. While never a huge fan of the Beats or their let-me-get-this-claptrap-down-before-my-heroin-dealer-gets-here prose, I thought it would make a fun gag gift for my father. ("They actually pay people to write this shit? I should be a fucking writer.")

At last, I could get my beloved bag and depart.

As I stood in the long, sloppy line that congealed at the register bank, an astonishing idea entered my head: What if I asked the cashier for *extra* bags? You know, backups. A reserve supply. It didn't mean I was committing to the bag for the rest of my life; I was just preparing for an extended period of internal debate.

Suddenly, I was startled by the ear-piercing command *"Next on line!"* and a not-so-gentle shove from the old fart behind me.

My heart sank as I approached the far register. It was manned by an icy-looking NYU grad student type whose hair was pulled back so severely she resembled some sort of predator fish. The young lady viciously swiped my credit card, flung it back at me, and bagged the book, all in one boorish flurry—as if *I'd* been the one who'd steered her toward a master's in social work when her true love had always been graphic design. With my window of opportunity closing, I seized the moment: "Um . . . would it be possible for me to get a few extra bags? I reuse them. To carry stuff."

She glowered at me with a mix of disdain and confusion, the same look she likely reserved for her older sister—the oncologist in Pound Ridge who's happily married and has always had her shit together. "I mean, I'll pay for them," I quickly added before she could say something curt, but of course saying something curt was her whole raison d'être.

"We don't *sell* the bags," she snipped. "And we don't give out extras." For a moment it seemed we were destined to tangle assholes, but a kindly woman with a manager's badge suddenly appeared and uttered seven of the sweetest words I'd ever heard in my life: "Oh, just give him the bags, Rachel." The next thing I knew, I was walking out of the store with *five* Strand bags—six if you count the one holding the Beat anthology. I was flying high.

It was about two blocks up Broadway that I realized something was wrong—my face started to feel numb and a disturbing buzz invaded my ear canals. The sidewalk began to slant and I had the vague sense that my skeletal frame was coming out of alignment. I braced myself against a building. A quick inspection of the new bag revealed the unthinkable: it had been redesigned. The handle opening was now slightly narrower and set about an inch lower from its former position. This completely threw off the balance and my gait suffered accordingly. Gone was the supportive ring of plastic on the interior, taking a good deal of comfort with it, and the bottom pleat was less pronounced, allowing the bag to bloat out grotesquely.

Once again, my long-held belief that tragedy lurks around every corner was confirmed. Something near and dear to me had been mutilated. A voice inside my head offered advice: "Track down the bag manufacturer! Locate the warehouse!

The older, better bags are still out there someplace! Be pro-active! And, P.S., everybody hates you."

I couldn't go on like this. The bag had robbed me of . . . well, I wasn't sure exactly what it robbed me of, but let's face it, it wasn't doing me any favors. For the sake of my family and everyone I cared about, I was done with it. There would be no calls of inquiry to bag manufacturers.

Suddenly I found myself engulfed in a wave of melancholy as the world around me began to darken and melt away. I could perceive nothing except for an odd, gesticulating mass of yellow on the southeast corner of Fourteenth Street—the same shade of yellow as the Strand bag. It was beckoning me.

I walked toward it.

The man in the chicken suit greeted me warmly, patting my shoulder with a shaky wing while thrusting a Popeyes menu in my hand. His black tights sagged hopelessly at his knees and a section of tattered beak revealed a runny nose. But it was those eyes—those cloudy milk-blue eyes peering out from the dented chicken head—that struck me. In them, I saw a stubborn pride.

The chicken man and I regarded each other for a moment, as if we had once traveled together across oceans and distant landforms. The moment soon passed, however, and he turned away, forcing a menu into the hand of an irritable gentleman who balled it up and called him a "bitch-ass-goofy-looking motherfucker." The bird did not flinch. Nor did he take off his chicken head and chuck it in the garbage. He simply moved on to the next pedestrian.

In that instant, I no longer cared what others thought of me. I was my own person. And I would never doubt myself again. I *was* the chicken man!

Slowly, the world around me returned. My head cleared. Sure, the new Strand bag was a bit of a mongrel, but heck, its virtues still outweighed its shortcomings. With a little duct tape I could reinforce the handles and some careful stretching would correct the alignment and improve balance. And Lorrie would figure out a way to fix the pleat—that's part of the reason I married her; she's so darn clever! I felt an enormous sense of pride. I was almost forty and beginning to grow as a person, learning to adapt to life's unexpected curveballs while maintaining my convictions. The bag was still mine. And I would carry it forever in *his* (the chicken guy's) honor. Do you hear that, gawkers? Do you hear that, Tumi messenger tote? In the words of the late Ben-Hur: "From my cold, dead hands!"

I continued my journey north as the rhythm of a slappy upright bass filled my head.

I'm traveling, brother. On the move. Crawling on all fours with muddy feet and twisted feathers. Impacted rubble stretching my bowels like a carny's tale of Aztec children. Creeps and sheep and lactating mothers pushing wheelbarrows full of passion nightmares who piss and shit and wail. The Empire State Building hunched against the wind like a dead man's erection. The bag, man, the bag. We build it up to fuck it up. I'm back on the train, daddy. Heading for that yawning cunt called the Upper West Side. Next stop . . . More of the Same.

Now scat.

The Lion in Winter

There was no need to check the caller ID. I knew it was him. I could tell by the ring—it grabbed you by the shoulders and spun you around. Even the phone seemed to panic, sprouting arms and legs and scurrying down the counter. "Pick it up! Pick it up!" it implored. "He hates to wait!"

"Hello?"

"Adam?"

"Hey, Dad."

"Okay, listen very carefully. Your mother bought a new cereal that's the best cereal I ever had in my life. It fortifies your whole body. You'll never eat another cereal again once you've had this. It's like eating a whole meal. In fact, I'm gonna have another bowl after we hang up."

"Wow, what's the name of it?"

"The name of what?"

"The cereal. What's it called?"

Brief pause. Obscure questions like this annoyed my father.

To himself: "Uh . . . what the hell. What's the goddamn thing called?" Then to me: "It's got a hell of a box. You should see all the literature on the back. It's very educational. It tells you everything about the human body. I'm just trying to remember the name of the damn thing . . . wait, hold on."

Muffled crushing sound. His "massive hands" (as he referred to them) were slaughtering the mouthpiece.

"Joyce?"

Beat.

"Joyce?"

Another beat.

"JOYCE!"

My mother, responding from a cave in Tora Bora, issued an unintelligible squawk.

"Adam's on the phone! He wants to know the name of that cereal!"

"Arrayrrrkkkk?" It was impossible to understand her. She was in the other room and the TV was blaring.

"The name of that cereal you bought!"

We were getting close to launch.

"Warrakkaa?"

"THE CEREAL! WHAT'S THE NAME OF THE FUCKING CEREAL?"

Liftoff.

"GODDAMN IT, DO I HAVE TO BUY A FUCKING BULLHORN TO HAVE A CONVERSATION WITH YOU? OR SHOULD I SEND UP SMOKE SIGNALS?"

He wearily apprised me of the situation: "Your poor mother's deaf as a fucking doornail, you know that, right? She makes Helen Keller look like a Rhodes Scholar." (Ostensibly suggesting that Helen Keller, along with her other difficulties, was retarded.)

Another yap from the cave. Merv responded in kind.

"NOT CREAM OF WHEAT! JESUS CHRIST, JOYCE! THE FUCKING CEREAL YOU BOUGHT THIS AFTERNOON! CAN YOU REMEMBER BACK THAT FAR?"

To me: "She won't be happy till she blows my voice box out. If you want to know the truth, she'd love to kill me. Then she can eat all the cereal she wants with her next husband. Hold on, let me get the box."

He dropped the phone on the counter. It slid off and

bounced on the floor a few times. I heard the sound of slamming cabinet doors and a snatch of conversation as my mother entered the room.

Joyce: "Calm down. It's right over there—two feet in front of your face."

Merv: "If your fucking brother wanted the cereal, you'd have it airlifted to him."

Joyce: "My brother doesn't eat cereal."

Some more rustling as the receiver made its bumpy pilgrimage back to his hand.

"Adam?"

"Yeah?"

"I got it right here. Just hold on . . ."

Beat.

"Let me look at this fucking thing . . ."

Pause.

"Okay, you there?"

"I am."

"It's called . . . [*slightly out of breath*] . . . Frosted Mini-Wheats."

Approximately six weeks later, the telltale ring sounded again. My startled telephone, frantic and disoriented, jumped

up and threw a pepper grinder through the kitchen window.
I ran in and lunged for the receiver.

"Hello?"

"Adam?"

"Hey, Dad."

"Now I want you to listen to me. You there?"

"Yes."

"Your mother bought some cookies today from Pathmark, and without any bullshit, it's gotta be the best cookie
I ever had in my life. They can't keep 'em on the shelves."

"Wow, really?"

"Anyone who buys another cookie oughta have their fucking head examined."

"What are they called?"

Silence.

"Uh . . . Christ, I just had 'em here . . ."

Beat.

"Joyce?"

Nothing.

"Joyce!"

Silence.

"JOYCE!"

From the other room: "Brayaak!"

"What's the name of those cookies?"

No response.

"The cookies you bought today! What are they called?"

"Brayaak?"

A beleaguered sigh gusts into my earpiece. "Adam, you have no idea what I go through in a single day. She's so fucking deaf. It wears me out. I can only take so much."

One more attempt.

"THE COOKIES! *WHAT THE FUCK IS THE NAME OF THE COOKIE?* FROM PATHMARK!"

He's back to me: "I was better off when I had bladder cancer. See, she's got those Weissman genes. They're all deaf . . . their hips go out . . . their knees go out. Her whole family's held together with Scotch tape."

"What about her new hearing aids?"

"Worthless. I feel sorry for the poor things. It's like trying to blast through concrete. Plus, she loses 'em all the time. See, it's a whole process here. I'm telling you, the average man couldn't take what I take."

My mother entered the room.

"Why are you yelling? You know I can't hear you from back there."

"You couldn't hear me if we were Siamese twins locked in a trunk."

"Don't give me nightmares."

"Look, I have Adam on the phone. He's in New York, okay? We're both tired and neither of us has time for this bullshit. What the hell are those new cookies called?"

"They're right there on the counter."

"How did they end up there?"

"That's where you put them."

"Oh. Okay"—into the receiver—"Adam, hold on a second."

He released the phone. Based on the sound I heard, it plummeted three thousand feet and landed on an oil drum. A bit of faint chatter followed.

Merv: "Where the hell were you hiding—the east wing? It's a fucking town house."

Joyce: "I was watching television. Next time walk in the room. You don't have to shout all the time."

Merv: "What's so important on television?"

Joyce: "Larry King."

Merv: "Jesus Christ, how can you watch that asshole?"

Joyce: "I like his guests."

Merv: "He looks like a fucking hemorrhoid."

Joyce: "Here, just take your cookies."

Rustling, a muffled word or two, the sound of a bag hitting the floor.

Merv: "Goddamn it! Hand me the fucking thing next time! I'm twenty feet away from you!"

Joyce: "I did. You dropped it."

Merv: "Ahh, go back to your box. Put on some cartoons, you'll like that."

Determined footsteps approached the phone and the receiver was reeled out of a gypsum quarry.

"Adam?"

"Yeah?"

"You still there?"

"Yup."

Crinkling paper in the background.

"Okay, I got the bag right here . . . where's the name of the goddamn things . . ."

More crinkling.

"Just sit tight."

"No problem."

"Okay, wait a second . . . you ready?"

"Yessir."

"All right, the name of the cookies are . . ."

Crinkle.

"Chip Ahoy . . . *Chunky.*"*

---

* Chunky Chips Ahoy! (Chip*s*—plural.)

A few weeks passed. It was evening. A series of pitched tones discharged from my new telephone—a stoic no-nonsense model that comported itself in a detached, almost business-like manner.

"Adam?"

"Hey, Dad, how's it going?"

"Do you have a minute?"

"Yeah, what's up?"

"Okay, well, your mother and I have decided we want to die together. I don't want to get morbid or anything, I'm just—did I interrupt your dinner?"

"No, no, I'm fine."

"Listen, we've been together a long time. I could never live without this woman. If, God forbid, she goes first, I'll blow my head off. I'm not trying to be dramatic—I'm just letting you know."

"Well, we don't have to think about this yet."

"And if I go first, I can promise you, she won't last long. She'll will herself to die. When you get to be our age, the bullshit's over. The best is behind you. There's no reason to—are you sure you're not eating?"

"Positive."

"Okay, now, point two: no fucking funeral and no Jews.

We want to be cremated and we want to go in the lake. You know, the lake behind the neighborhood here."

"Right, I know."

"I want you to be the honcho on this."

"Okay."

"So here's how it works: Whoever dies first, they get incinerated and put in the closet. When the second one goes, mix us together and put us in the lake. Now, if your mother goes first, be patient, because I'll blow my head off."

"We won't have to deal with this for a long time . . ."

"And I want the cat in there too."

"You want the cat in where?"

"I want the cat cremated and mixed in with us."

"Oh. So Mom's okay with that?"

"Hey, she knows what that cat means to me. Here, ask her yourself."

He called for my mother.

"Joyce!"

A hush.

"Joyce!"

Radio silence.

"JOYCE!"

She hollered back from the laundry room: *"What?"*

"Adam's on the phone! Tell him about the cat!"

"What about the cat?"

"The ashes! When we're dead!"

"I don't care! Whatever makes you happy!"

Merv (*to me*): "Did you hear that, Adam?"

Me: "Yup. Sounds like she rubber-stamped it."

My father chuckled and called out to her again: "Adam said you rubber-stamped it!"

Joyce: "I stamped what?"

Merv: "The cat!"

Joyce: "What about the cat?"

Merv: "Never mind! It's like talking to the fucking lamp!" To me: "I told you she lost her hearing aid again, didn't I? They have a shrine to her at the hearing aid factory. Listen, once we're all dead, mix me, your mother, and the cat together. Then put us in the lake. Right by the birdfeeders."

I heard footsteps in the background.

"Here comes Seattle Slew. They built the Panama Canal in the time it takes her to move her ass from one room to the other."

Joyce: "Can't you walk back to me instead of yelling?"

"For Christ's sake, Joyce, I'm telling Adam about the lake!" Back to me: "Adam, by the way, remember—no ceremony and no Jews."

I egged him on a bit for my own amusement.

"But Pop, you don't want to insult your fellow congregants, do you? What will they say at the temple?"

"Fuck them and the temple."

Still having fun with it: "But, *Daddy*, I always heard Jews stuck together."

"Whoever told you that's been reading too many comic books. If I told you half the shit I went through growing up, you'd vomit."

My mother picked up the other phone: "Not all Jewish people are like that. Adam, don't get him started."

It was too late.

"They basically killed my grandfather. Can you imagine? He was one of the most respected rabbis in Russia, and he gets over here and has to work in a fucking butcher shop."

"Unbelievable," I commented on the oft-told story.

"We were so fucking poor I had rickets. My sister too. We couldn't afford milk. And he's killing chickens in a butcher shop. See, the European Jews looked down on the Russian Jews."

"Did the Russian Jews stick together at least?"

"Maybe in outer space. These bastards, they'd come in to pick up their chickens from my grandfather and it was always the same shit [*mimicking a Yiddish accent*]: 'This is not my chicken. The chicken I brought you was much larger than this chicken.'"

"Ha-ha."

"All day long. 'This is not my chicken.' I would've shoved the chicken up their ass."

Joyce: "I bet you never heard that one before, Adam."

"Well, it's interesting. It clearly had an effect on Dad."

"Then they made me get rid of my dog. [*Yiddish accent*]: 'A *shochet* should not have animals in the house. Animals are dirty.' Meanwhile, their fucking beards are full of—aw, fuck it."

"Crazy."

"That dog was the only friend I had."

Joyce: "Well, that's how they were back then. They were old-fashioned."

Merv: "I got no use for any of 'em."

Me: "Sucks."

Merv: "So, make sure we're mixed together real good, the cat too. I don't know how you do it, but you'll find some literature."

Me: "So you're okay with the cat, Mom?"

Joyce: "If it makes your father happy."

Merv: "Listen, Adam, we've only been married sixty years. If that's not love, everyone can go fuck themselves. I mean, next to us, Romeo and Juliet were a couple of assholes."

Joyce: "Can't you find a nicer way of saying it?"

Merv: "We were just kids, for Christ's sake. All the Jews

said it wouldn't last. They said she was pregnant. Meanwhile, we're still together and they're all dead."

Me: "It's quite a love story."

"I almost had a heart attack the first time I laid eyes on your mother she was so beautiful. I didn't have a penny to my name. She's gotta be the kindest human being who ever lived."

Me: "I agree."

"She makes Jesus Christ look like a prick."

Joyce: "That's awful. Don't say that."

"Adam, let me put it to you this way—if anyone ever touched her, I'd put 'em in the fucking cemetery."

"You always made that clear."

"So, listen, the next time you're in town I'll show you the spot. You know the lake behind the buildings? Right by the big tree there. Just dump us in."

"Okay, but there's no rush. Nobody's going anywhere."

"Look, the Bible, if you go for that crap, says *threescore and ten*, so I already got 'em fucked by nine. I don't have to be a pig about it."

"Yeah, I guess . . ."

"But I will not live without your mother."

"I understand."

A pause. Some decompression. The topic had run its course.

Me: "Anyway, what else is new? Still eating those Frosted Mini-Wheats?"

Merv: "Eating what?"

"That cereal you like."

"What cereal?"

"Frosted Mini-Wheats—you know, those little shredded wheat things. They fortify your whole body. Remember?"

"Oh, those. Ha. No, those are pure shit."

"Wow. Seems like you were just telling me not that long ago how much you liked them."

"Well, I used to believe in Santa Claus, too."

A Fork in the Midway

The infant was born on the cusp of winter as dawn rose on the twentieth century. Its sick jangly cry whipped across the frigid river and twisted its way through the mills and factories where, for a heartbeat, production of steel and aluminum seemed to halt. Outside the tiny house, a passerby might have observed distressed figures swimming in the dull yellow light behind the soiled window. They hovered around him, frightened and praying, as the broken little boy struggled to prove himself worthy of life.

Some time later, far away, another child entered the world. Fleshy and full of want, it sang out, strong and greedy, as if it hoped to devour the earth itself. Those in attendance conveyed obligatory smiles and bland compliments to the exhausted mother. Yet there was an uneasiness in the room. No one dared speak of it, but these were clearly the cries of an asshole.

My tenth-grade American History class was informed that we would be missing the second half of school on Tuesday to watch a threshing machine demonstration at the York Fair. Within moments of the announcement, I'd already formulated a plan: I would sneak off from the group and go to the freak show. In a weak moment, I invited Roy Hatcher to come along, but he balked—not because he feared getting caught, but because he felt it was wrong. Roy Hatcher, apparently, was in school to learn—and skipping off to see people with birth defects was not his idea of a good time. I had to shake my head. Just another shallow fuck who didn't get it.

I was mad about freaks in those days, absorbing every poetic metaphor and lofty allegory that writers of freak books tossed my way. They were indeed "very special people," and I—a perfectly healthy albeit freakishly pale-skinned boy from the gritty pastures of Pennsylvania Dutch Country—*related* to them. I, too, was an outcast: I saw things differently! Felt things more deeply! I refused to run with the pack, and the pack had no interest in running with me. (I forget which came first.) And if all that wasn't divergent enough, I didn't like the movie *Animal House*.

My true place, I was convinced, was among my brethren in the congress of living curiosities, and a trip to the York Fair was my pilgrimage to Jerusalem. I never missed a season back then and consider myself privileged to have met some of the greats in their twilight years: Esther the Alligator Girl, conjoined twins Ronnie and Donnie, Toad Boy Otis Jordan (who later tinkered with his act and rechristened himself "The Human Cigarette Factory"), and how could I forget the talkative black midget in a pinstripe suit whose name escapes me (as the names of midgets often do), who in one long exhale took me through his entire career—from his days of dancing on the sidewalk for chestnuts to appearing on the great vaudeville stages alongside such notables as Sophie Tucker and "Sleep 'n' Eat." (A career virtually identical to that of a white midget I once met who also danced for chestnuts and worked with Sophie Tucker and Percy Kilbride from the Ma and Pa Kettle films.)

But it's all gone now. Disability groups, handicap associations, and other like-minded busybodies have succeeded in closing the sideshows down, armed with nothing more than common sense and a just cause. Walk into a "Human Oddity" tent these days and what passes for a freak is probably a guy without tattoos who abhors social media.

The history teacher, Mr. Mueller, was a known boozehound, wife beater, and antique tractor buff. Two-thirds of that explained our field trip to see a nineteenth-century thresher demonstration. Had we been on point with our current studies, we'd be eating Quarter Pounders at the

McDonald's in Gettysburg. Mueller shooed us off the bus and gave us our directives: "Keep your asses moving and your traps shut!" It was just the Dewar's talking, but still . . . poor Mrs. Mueller.

The heart of the fair and all its glories loomed beyond us as we were frog-marched to that ground zero of tedium: the exhibition and livestock buildings. Somewhere, not very far away, was a girlie show, but where we walked, there was only erection-dousing signage with come-ons like EMBROIDERY AND CROCHET and BLACKSMITH VS. COBBLER! And everywhere—*everywhere*—the smell of shit.

We entered the Tools and Agriculture Annex and rubbed elbows with the other hostages—dead-eyed 4-H'ers, confused nursing home captives, and the A-list from the state hospital. One of my classmates, Brenda Strode, recognized her uncle in the latter group and waved excitedly, but he was getting yelled at for breaking a cheese press.

"A testament to the ingenuity of modern man!" a John Deere salesman decreed as we stood before an evolving display of cutting implements that commenced with a sharp rock and climaxed with a riding mower. Mr. Mueller allowed us a few moments to gawk at the sickles before hustling everyone outside to the Main Event—the T. rex of the tour: the steam thresher. We gathered around an old Gomer who said something about wheat, the 1800s, and boilers, while occasionally hawking a chunk of his respiratory system into a paisley scarf. I made sure to raise my hand so my attendance would be noted.

"Uh . . . how big are those tires?" I queried, in a voice choked with fascination.

Mr. Mueller fielded that one: "They're wheels, not tires, you idiot!"

"Oh, yeah, I meant 'wheels.'"

"Resnick—shut up!"

Mission accomplished. Then the old man fired up the tractor, which made a god-awful racket in the predictable nineteenth-century manner, and the entire class was swallowed up in a cloud of steam. I saw my window. By the time the thresher lurched forward, I was running through the Swine and Poultry Building, out a side door, and into the heart of the midway, where my senses quickly engaged in a turf war over the bomb blast of stimuli: racing pigs, fried lard, the distant voice of Eddie Rabbitt singing "Two Dollars in the Jukebox" from the grandstand, competing with the furious growl of a preacher holding a microphone to his mechanical larynx . . . and hey, was that a tattoo of David Duke on that guy's arm? *Keep moving, don't make eye contact. Yonder lies the temple.*

The banners flapping outside the sideshow tent were worrisome, indicating more than a few "working acts" and animal fluff. I was there to see real human oddities, not a sword swallower, not the Human Blockhead, and certainly not that bovine snooze-fest Pixie the Mini Cow. Luckily, there was one banner that stood out from the rest and justified my reason for being there. I entered the tent as the Human Blockhead was going into his big closer—hammering a railroad spike up his left nostril. Those hoping to see a gush of blood and snot were to be sorely disappointed; this man was a professional. After some cornball patter about clearing his sinuses "the old-fashioned way," he pried the spike from his nose and was warmly received by the crowd. My timing was fortuitous. The spectators were then invited to meet the performers, who were lined up on a long platform like monarchs whose kingdom was second only to Eddie Rabbitt's trailer.

Sideshow folk were always happy to greet their public, but even happier to sell you a "pitch card"—a small photograph depicting their unique talents or unusual appearance. Over the course of a season, they could make some decent money selling these souvenirs, although I suspect Pixie the Mini Cow got fucked over by her manager. Being a purist, I knew there was only one card worth getting that day, and boy was it a peach.

Sealo the Seal Boy wasn't hard to spot—he was sitting in a little chair toward the end of the platform, wearing a smile that lit up the entire tent (the cigar dangling precariously from his mouth threatened to do the same). Far from being a boy, he appeared to be a man in his sixties, pleasant-looking and utterly unremarkable in every regard, despite having no arms, and hands that protruded from his shoulders. He may not have lived on an ice floe or encountered the puzzled gapes of sea lions as depicted on the banner outside, but Sealo was a genuine, bona fide freak.

"Hi, there! What's your name?" he said as I approached the platform.

"Adam Resnick," I replied with starstruck formality.

"Nice to meet you, Adam!" he beamed. Sealo offered his hand and I reached up and shook it. It was a little disconcerting, but still more pleasant than kissing a few of my aunts. Somehow his physical characteristics weren't as jarring as I expected, and quite frankly, he kind of pulled it off. Certainly better than I could have. Sealo was a cool guy.

"Where ya from, Adam?"

"Harrisburg."

"Oh, I've been through there. You're right by Chocolate Town. I went through the factory, you know. That was years ago. They had those big tanks full of chocolate . . . man, I wanted to jump right in!"

He laughed and the cigar danced around on his lips. I felt lousy about it, but the image of Sealo swimming in chocolate did take some of the fun out of Hershey bars for a while.

"Do you do good in school, Adam?" he asked, turning serious.

"No, not really," I replied, unable to lie to him.

"Well, I understand," he said, "school might not seem like such a hot deal right now, but you'll be amazed where it'll take you in life. Learning is probably the most important thing a fellow can do for himself. What do you want to be?"

"I don't know," I answered. "I never really thought about it."

"That's all right, you'll sort it out. I'm not worried about you at all. I know my customers!"

It was the first time in my life that someone had expressed anything remotely like hope for me. In that sense, Sealo really was a freak. He saw me differently than I saw myself.

People were starting to push in now, waiting to meet the Seal Boy, but I didn't want to leave; I wanted to exchange phone numbers, make plans to hang out, get to know his family. I needed this guy in my life. I could imagine Sealo in a Santa Claus suit, soothing the minds of neurotic children everywhere, dispensing insight and encouragement—providing *hope*. Then I envisioned the horrified faces of those same children trying to squirm out of his lap, their outraged parents, and the angry mall manager screaming at the guy who'd hired Sealo in the first place: "He's got no fucking arms! Broom him!"

Block it out, I told myself. Be positive. Have faith in people. Wasn't that ultimately Sealo's message?

I bought several of his pitch cards: Sealo shaving, Sealo holding a hunting rifle, Sealo sawing a piece of lumber— Sealo doing, doing, doing. Sans *arms.* What did that make me? What would my pitch cards depict? Adam complaining, Adam making excuses, Adam raging and bitter.

I respectfully asked him to sign one of the cards, and he did so with great care and deliberation.

"Adam, it was a real pleasure to meet you," he said, passing the card back to me. "I'll be keeping an eye out for you."

I bid my new friend farewell and moved onward. The world seemed twice as big now, awash with possibility, if only I allowed myself to see it. And then, suddenly, there I was: standing below Big Ben, a 650-pound man packed into a redwood lawn chair with a doomed vinyl pillow lodged beneath him. His head was tilted back and his eyes were closed. His lips, pressed into fierce lines, echoed the creases in his forehead. A handwritten sign, crafted from a piece of cardboard that still retained a portion of the Birds Eye logo, was propped up next to him. Its message was direct and uncere-monious: DON'T ASK ME QUESTIONS—I HAVE A SORE THROAT.

My outrage came quickly. Just a few yards away sat Sealo—a real freak—giving his all, while this fat piece of shit clocked out due to a scratchy throat. How dare he even breathe the same sawdust! What happened to "the show must go on"? I immediately sized up Big Ben for what he was: an interloper, a charlatan, a pox on the Congress of Liv-ing Curiosities. He was the anti-Sealo. Yet it was so much more than that. Big Ben, ladies and gentlemen, was a testa-ment to the worthlessness of modern man.

A little farm boy wandered over, perhaps eight or nine years old, so nondescript he looked familiar. He squinted at the uncommunicative fat turd on the patio chair and then looked at me, as if seeking confirmation. I gestured toward the sign, and he read it, lips moving silently. A scowl came across his face. He stepped closer to the platform and grunted.

"Hey! Fat Ben!" he called out.

I flinched.

"Hey, fatso, how come you don't talk?"

In direct noncompliance of the cardboard sign, he had asked Big Ben a question! But Ben did not stir, save for a small twitch in his left pinky, which I may have imagined. The boy muttered to himself, "He ain't really sleepin'."

He kicked the platform, producing a loud hollow thud. I almost ran out of the tent.

"You know you ain't really sleepin'!" he cried out. "Why'd you take my money if you ain't gonna talk?"

The kid showed no signs of wrapping up his interrogation. But it wasn't my business. I was merely a bystander.

"How big are your underpants, fatty?" he continued. "I bet your mother was a cow. Is that why you're so damn fat? Do you moo like a cow? Do you shit in the yard like a cow?" The boy deserved a lot of credit, but to suggest that Big Ben was anything like a cow was an insult to the diminutive Pixie, who was corralled nearby eating grain from a teacup.

I decided to help the kid refine his line of questioning. He was missing the whole point.

"Ask him if he understands the word 'obligation,'" I whispered. "Explain that real freaks abide by a code of principles. Ask him if he's ever danced in the street for chestnuts or inspired a single human being in his entire—"

A loud crack suddenly reverberated through the tent; it sounded like a branch snapping off a tree during a storm.

Big Ben's chair had shifted.

Like a great, horrible creature in a Ray Harryhausen film, the fat man slowly came to life. One eye sluggishly opened, followed by the other. An expulsion of air passed through his dead lips, which swiftly filled with color. There were creaks and groans as the chair shuddered beneath him. He then slowly rose, like a bloated Neptune ascending from the sea. Up, up he went, as curtains of flab jiggled and unfurled from every extremity. Big Ben towered above us now, gazing down at the boy from the edge of the platform. His chest heaved and a drop of perspiration formed in the cleft of his chin.

Thank God my hands are clean on this one, I thought.

That's when his ruddy tomato-shaped face swiveled in my direction, where it would remain. With the arrogance of a peacock presenting its tail, Ben extended his meaty arm, revealing a constellation of psoriasis plaques. A sausage-like finger pointed at my forehead.

"There's a man knocking at your front door!" he thundered in a rich, full voice without the slightest hint of throat irritation. "And that man's name is Jesus Christ!" My skin suddenly felt prickly. I glanced over, ready to blame the kid, but he was gone.

A small crowd began to gather.

"This prideful, selfish boy," he boomed, finger still jabbing at my face, "is *lost*. Failed by his minister, failed by his parents . . . failed by *each and every one of us!*"

A few folks murmured in agreement and I suddenly longed to be at the threshing demonstration.

"He lives by his own set of rules. He cares for no one but

himself. The whole of human civilization is his to laugh at. But his foot will slide in due time!"

Big Ben brought his gaze back to me where I remained frozen, fixated on that huge flabby arm—an arm with enough flesh for ten limbs, an embarrassment of riches.

"The choice is yours, boy—two paths! Sin or God! Sin or God! *Sin or God!*" Each pronouncement went up an octave; the final one was so cracked and high-pitched it was barely audible. I could feel every syllable in my throat, as if I'd swallowed a nest of tangled wires.

And with that, the fattest man in York, Pennsylvania, collapsed back in his chair. The vinyl pillow hissed, getting in the last word.

When I rejoined my classmates, they were sitting in a field by the exhibition buildings, enjoying apple cider and cake donuts. Mr. Mueller was still inspecting the thresher, driving the farmer nuts with redundant questions about a throttle valve. I sat on the ground by a small shed, away from the others, leaning against a discarded sign that simply said BOILED! in red milk paint.

Roy Hatcher wandered over.

"Well, did you see your freaks?" he asked, looking down at me.

"No. I didn't go."

"Then where were you?"

"I didn't go anywhere."

He gave me an odd look and walked back to his place among the donut eaters.

I was watching a pair of resigned-looking mules being loaded into a trailer when a shadow fell over me. I looked up and saw Mr. Mueller.

"You think I'm an idiot, Resnick?" he demanded.

"No."

"You think I'm too dumb to do a head count?"

"No."

"See me first thing tomorrow or I'll have your ass wrapped in cellophane. This shit won't fly, you know that, right?"

So many questions. How do people deal with so many questions?

When it comes to guilt, I'm an easy lay. I have a habit of believing only the bad things that are said about me. And Big Ben obviously knew me inside out. He had my number all right, that listless fat fuck. Or did I have his? Could truthful words be spoken in a voice that was itself a lie? Did Big Ben really have a sore throat? In considering the notion that the world was divided between the Sealos and the Big Bens, where did I fit in?

My head was starting to pound, and I wondered, as I often did, if I had mental problems.

I reached into my pocket for Sealo's pitch card and read the inscription:

To Adam—a swell fellow. Always remember your visit to the York Fair.

Boy Refuses to Hold
Frozen Turkey

Ever since I was a toddler, I've had a distaste for self-promotion. I would no sooner tell some jackass "what a doggie says" than specify where my belly button was—or any other body part for that matter. Some of this stemmed from a congenital low threshold for embarrassment, and the rest can be chalked up to my basic revulsion for human interaction. By the time I was seven or so, my mother decided this behavior was no longer cute. The turning point, I believe, came during a trip to the grocery store, when I was offered the opportunity to appear on the front page of the *Patriot-News*, holding a frozen turkey with cash stuffed in my mouth.

The exact concept behind the picture remains unclear to

this day. It obviously had something to do with Thanksgiving—that much the principals agree on—but there's still some debate whether the man worked for the newspaper or the supermarket. And I've yet to find a satisfying connection between holding a turkey and biting down on money. In the end, all that mattered was that he found me. I was standing alone at the magazine rack, minding my own business, leafing through a copy of *Famous Monsters of Filmland*.

The photographer wore round Harold Lloyd glasses and was holding one of those old-fashioned press cameras with the big flash reflector. He looked like just about every guy my father knew: skinny tie, wingtips, and a head full of Wildroot. There was a little bounce in his eyebrows that he probably used to greater effect with pretty waitresses.

"Hey, son, is your mother around?"

Everything seemed to move at the speed of light. Joyce dashed over with her shopping cart like a community theater player whose entrance screamed OVEREAGER! There was a brightness in her eyes, as if she knew something extraordinary was about to happen, maybe the greatest thing to happen in the history of the Resnick family.

The photographer laid it out for her: "I want to put this monkey in the *Patriot*, whaddaya think, Mom? He's gonna hold a frozen turkey, we'll put some cash in his mouth, it's gonna be beautiful."

"In the *Patriot*?" she responded, coaxing him to repeat it.

"Right on the front page—the boy, the bird, the dough . . . it'll be gorgeous."

"But he's got such a dirty face." She giggled, sounding like a freshman sneaking her first smoke in the lavatory.

"I love the dirty face! He's all boy! Give me the messy hair too!" He locked my head in his arm like a TV wrestler and mussed up my hair. I wanted to kill him.

They both laughed. I unconsciously rolled the magazine into a tube, tightening my fist around Peter Cushing's throat. Had I been asked, I would've let it be known that I couldn't think of anything more repulsive than having my picture in the newspaper. Beyond the props, beyond the notion of putting filthy, grimy money in my mouth for reasons that had yet to be explained, how absurd to think I'd agree to put myself on display, to allow people to see my face and read my name. Forget the embarrassment of it all; what if someone recognized me in public and said "Hi"? Christ, I didn't want to meet anyone new. Between school and other activities beyond my control, I had enough fucking people in my life.

"So here's what we'll do," the photographer plowed ahead, "we'll set him up over there, below the manager's booth and we'll hang a flag behind him. It'll be tremendous!"

What the hell is he talking about?

"And we'll get a stack of tens and twenties and he'll clamp

down on 'em. You know, really chomp down and show the cabbage."

Joyce shrugged as if she had no choice in the matter, chirping, "Oh well, I guess you're the boss!" No questions, no "Let me think it through"—just run with it. Sure, the kid'll look like an asshole, but hey—it's going on the front page!

The photographer whistled to the store manager, who jumped up in his elevated booth like a startled hen. He seemed to be half asleep and shaking off a nightmare. Straightening his smock and bow tie, he grabbed the microphone and announced over the PA: "Meat Department—bird, ten pound, frozen, up front, picture." Later, in third grade, I thought back to that sentence when we were learning about verbs.

My mother squeezed my shoulders.

"Isn't this exciting? Out of all the kids, he picked you!"

Poor Joyce. So swept up in the moment that she'd lost all sense of reality and forgotten who she was dealing with. Or maybe she thought if she could distract me long enough, I wouldn't realize what was happening until it was too late.

"Did you hear the Keeners got a Chow Chow?" she asked. "What was the name of their old dog again? The one with the little wheels on his back legs?"

"I'm not doing it," I said, casting the monster magazine into the shopping cart. "I want to wait in the car."

She took a deep breath and knelt down, stroking my hair in a funny direction so it remained messy.

"It's just a picture, sweetie. It'll be over in two seconds."

I resented the patronizing logic. I wasn't four years old anymore and this wasn't a tetanus shot. Certainly she had to be aware by now of my astonishing power to foresee every conceivable downside to a situation. And this little caper—which I would never consent to under any circumstance—wasn't going to vanish in a flash of magnesium. The fallout would be long and grisly:

"Hey, Adam, saw your picture in the paper."

"There he is! Mr. Picture in the Paper!"

"That was a heck of a turkey you were holding in that picture, in the paper."

"Lemme ask ya, kid, what was the point of the money in your mouth?"

No thank you. Give me tetanus, give me diphtheria, give me that weird disease that turns kids into old people, but I wanted no part of this jackpot.

The photographer sensed something was off. He asked my mother if there was a problem. She responded with a shy parlor laugh like a Tennessee Williams character.

"No, just a silly little boy is all. They can be positively *willful* at this age. Ha-ha."

She grabbed my arm and pulled me aside.

"Not everything is about *you*," she hissed. "This man is being very nice and he was probably in the war and the least you can do is be cooperative!"

I was nothing if not diplomatic. I told her the guy was welcome to take my picture as long as it didn't involve a turkey, the American flag, or soiled currency in my mouth. Additionally, it could not appear in the newspaper or any other publication. A look of unbridled fury came over her. She plucked *Famous Monsters of Filmland* from the shopping cart and flung it back toward the magazine rack, where it fluttered like a bat before dying behind the stamp machine. "What makes you think you deserve that book? What makes you think you deserve anything! I do so much for you, and this one time, all I ask for is—"

She quickly composed herself and tried a different approach—offering to take me to the hobby shop to buy the Invisible Man model I wanted so badly. I responded favorably to the suggestion . . . with the caveat that it wouldn't require me to pose for a picture that appeared in the newspaper or any other publication. She did a "slow burn"—or as I recognized it, the face Moe makes right before he throttles Curly.

A pudgy little man with the face of a dull child arrived clutching a frozen turkey. His white apron was mottled with blood the same color as his name tag, which was blank. He shuffled over to the manager's booth and held the turkey high in the air. The manager snapped, "Don't give it to me, you moron! Give it to the kid!" The little man walked the turkey over to me, but I turned away, refusing it. Then he carted it back to his boss, reporting in a weepy voice, "But he don't want it neither." The annoyed manager looked up from his clipboard and replied, "What do you mean, *He don't want it neither?* Of course he wants it!" "I tried to give it to him," the little man explained, "but he won't put his hands or arms out or nothin'."

The photographer was growing concerned. He glanced at my mother and simply said, "Ma'am?" Joyce looked like she wanted to crawl under the display of Campfire marshmallows and die. Finally, she mumbled, "He said he doesn't want to do it."

"Doesn't want to do it? Doesn't want to do *what?*" He seemed genuinely baffled. Who in their right mind would refuse an opportunity like this?

The manager grunted and stomped down the four steps from his roost, emerging through a low swinging door. He grabbed the turkey from the little man—scaring him half to death—and marched over to me. His eyes softened and he concocted a smile.

"Whattsa matter, Sarge? You don't wanna hold the turkey?" I didn't answer. "You know what—I just might let you *keep* that turkey." He eyed the photographer and repeated, "I just might let him keep that son of a gun!" The photographer ran with it: "Wow. It's a big one too. I bet a strong boy like him could hold that buzzard like it was a pack of cigarettes." He winked at my mother, who blatantly begged, "Adam, *pleeease* hold the turkey."

The photographer squatted down and tried to look me in the eye.

"This is going on the front page, son. Everyone's gonna see it—your friends, your family, old grandpops . . . imagine that." The manager reached into his smock and withdrew a wad of limp bills. He grinned broadly, pointed to the money, then to his mouth, and finally at me, miming some magnificent concept he felt I wasn't grasping. I responded by gazing down at an ancient produce sticker that appeared fused to the linoleum, marveling at how it survived all these years.

"He's just so willful," my dazed mother said to no one in particular.

The photographer sighed and spoke to the back of my head. "Are you sure about this, son? Don't you want to make Mom happy?"

Del Monte Quality Banano de Costa Rica.

"Son, are you listening?"

Moments later I was trailing behind my mother as she finished her shopping. She was walking unusually fast and my corduroys were swooshing like a wind turbine. Every box, jar, and sack was viciously hurled into the cart, and I noticed the back of her neck looked sunburned. All the cute shit, like calling me her "number one helper" or "the best tomato-picker-outer in the world," was absent, replaced by dead air and an icy disregard. I wisely kept my mouth shut. I think it pissed her off more.

My brother Rick found us. Five years older than me, he was allowed to wander around the shopping center alone and even play pinball at the bowling alley across the street. Now he was irritated, wanting to go home and wondering why my mother hadn't checked out yet. "Why don't you ask your brother?" she suggested, ratting me out. I gave up nothing, of course, so it was her pleasure to unburden herself of the details. Naturally, I was portrayed as the bad guy, but her retelling of the events was needlessly emotional and riddled with inaccuracies. For one thing, at no point had I "thrown a fit" and I certainly wasn't "tossing magazines around like a crazy person." *She's* the one who threw the magazine.

"You stupid idiot!" Rick screamed in my face. "You could've been in the paper! That money was yours to keep! Who cares if it was in your mouth? It was probably hundreds of dollars!" As usual, he had it all figured out.

Ever the opportunist, Rick rushed off to find the photographer. This was a kid who craved the spotlight. Whether it was at school, Little League, or the Blue Mountain chapter of the Good Deed Bandits, he was constantly looking for a way to put himself out there. This time, though, he came up empty. The photographer was at Woolworth's, still on the prowl for a cute kid with a dirty face, when Rick tracked him down. My brother did everything he could to charm and bullshit his way into the gig, rattling off one good deed after another, but he was just too old. He wasn't "right." The photographer wanted *me*. There was just one problem: He couldn't have me. Not for all the fame and fortune he could ram down my throat. And why? Because I didn't do things like that.

On the ride home, Joyce and Rick talked in the front seat like they were the only people in the car.

"He's got problems," Rick told her. "He doesn't even have any friends. Do you know how many friends I had at his age? Remember the time I got everyone to sign up for the bike rodeo? Best year ever. Remember the picture they put up—me giving the coffee can to the March of Dimes guy?"

"He has a good heart," my mother said. "He just gets in his own way sometimes."

"Kids hate kids like him. *I* would hate him. It's only a matter of time before he gets beat up."

Thanksgiving morning, the newspaper banged against the screen door. Rick ran out to get it. On the front page was a picture of Walter DeCanto holding a frozen turkey. There were a few wrinkled bills lodged between his nubby teeth. The caption below said something about "Thanksgiving Savings." Walter was a grade ahead of me. I didn't really know him, but my mother always claimed that his mother "acted entitled." So that added a nice little patina to things.

Dinner that evening was quiet for a Resnick Thanksgiving. No screaming, no violence—even my father was unusually sedate. There was an unspoken feeling in the dining room that we had lost out on something, and would continue to lose out. We would never be front-pagers. And that was just fine with me. I was the invisible man.

The Sensodyne Lady

The Kid wanted to play the piano. I tried to wise her to the facts: no Resnick had ever been able to play a musical instrument, or, for that matter, to draw, sing, or produce anything of beauty. I mapped it all out for her—how she'd dread the lessons, get frustrated by her lack of ability, and inevitably quit. No Resnick, I reiterated, will ever, *ever* be able to play the piano. That's how much I loved this little girl. But she was seven. She was a kid. And kids live in lollipop land.

I had the same pipe dream when I was about her age. I wanted to pound out that old-time jazzy stuff I heard in black-and-white cartoons—songs like "Let's Do It," "Hard-to-Get Gertie," and "No Wonder She's a Blushing Bride." It took only one piano lesson to knock me in line. "Certainly you didn't expect to just sit down and be able to play, did you?" asked the baffled piano teacher. Well, as a matter of fact, yes I did, honey. I'd seen mice, ducks, and even a porcupine do it, why the fuck *not me*? Now I had to protect my daughter from the same wake-up call. Or maybe, subconsciously, I wanted to prevent her from succeeding at something I had failed at. That's not such a bad thing, right? Just human nature.

Ultimately, though, there was a larger issue—I didn't want a piano in the apartment. They're big ugly things, those pianos. Dust catchers. And unlike rabbits or tropical fish, they never die. Your family dies around it. The piano always gets the last laugh. My wife, Lorrie, the normal one, told me to take a deep breath. We didn't have to get a *real* piano, she explained, just one of those digital keyboards. They're only a few hundred bucks and you can shove it under the bed.

I'm not an unreasonable man. I could live with that. And maybe the Kid needed to learn about failure. She'd had an easy ride up to this point.

We bought the fake piano, but the piano teacher didn't like fake pianos. Something about the keys not being weighted. What we needed, she told us—in front of the Kid—was a real piano. Thanks for having my back, Hot Asian Girl. I guess all that giggling at my witty asides wasn't you being flirty after all. It was out of my hands. Like finding yourself in the path of a freight train or a junked-up mistress with a straight razor, I was outmaneuvered by destiny. I left the piano shopping to Lorrie, requesting only that it not be one of those nursing home models.

It wasn't long before she had "amazing" news: a woman in the building was selling her piano and wanted only a hundred dollars for it. The porters had already checked it out and said it would be easy to move. It was all too perfect and too fast. I wanted to know more. First, who was the seller?

"The lady on eight," Lorrie said. "She's got black frizzy hair. The one with the blind schnauzer?" I made it my business not to look at or interact with anyone in the building, so this triggered nothing.

"You know, she was in the Sensodyne commercial."

I was still blindfolded and the piñata was across the street.

"Remember her husband—the really nice man with the cane, the one who died? He was on chemo? You hated the way he was always whistling?"

That vaguely rang a bell. I moved on to the important issue: What did this piano look like?

It was an upright, she said, not the coolest-looking thing in the world, but not awful. It was the right size and would do the job. Plus, the Kid liked it. I detected a bit of salesmanship in her voice. The whole thing seemed to just fall out of the sky. I insisted on seeing it.

She was bony, with firm, stringy muscles, and had no business wearing a tank top. Her Bellevue eyes complemented the wild salt-and-pepper hair that was straight out of a fright-wig catalog, or perhaps one of Darwin's early sketchbooks. She appeared to be in her late fifties and was a quintessential New York loon—one of those classic Upper West Side ladies who smiled too much, had intergalactic notions about the existence of man, yet fiercely observed the High Holidays. I looked around the apartment. It was all there—the clutter, the framed Metropolitan Opera print, the brigade of Solgar vitamin bottles, and the funk of vegan pork. How this woman ever wound up in a toothpaste commercial must have been quite a story, one I had absolutely no interest in.

Her first words were to Lorrie and they were weighted with disappointment: "Oh, *this* is your husband?" Obviously she'd seen me around the building and wasn't a fan. Perhaps I had insulted her somewhere along the line. Maybe she accidentally pushed the wrong floor on the elevator once and heard me exhale obnoxiously—a response I often produce for screwheads who waste three seconds of my valuable time. It didn't matter. I was there on business, not to mend fences.

Lorrie, as it turned out, had been kind in her description of the piano. It was possibly the ugliest contrivance ever built by white men, to borrow an unpleasant phrase from Mr. Houck, my ninth-grade shop teacher. It reeked of the early sixties, with its piss-yellow wood and fancy curves. No matter where my eye wandered, it was assaulted by filigree, lattice-work, or "what the fuck, let's give it a shot" ornamentation. My best theory was that it had been designed to coax orgasms out of grieving old ladies who went piano shopping after the Kennedy assassination. Simply put, it wasn't to my taste.

I tried to extract my wife from the apartment, but the woman had her pinned down. Her eyes grew damp as she nattered away about the piano and how all her kids learned to play on it, and she didn't have room for it anymore because her sick mother was moving in, and how she prayed and prayed it would find a happy home. Who or what she prayed to was anyone's guess; I pictured a metallic space crab with female breasts and a penis, wearing a yarmulke. But there was something more disturbing afoot here: She appeared to be under the impression that this was a done deal. Surely she couldn't be that batty, I thought. "Oh, I'm so grateful!" she announced, walking past me to hug Lorrie. Her shoulder blades stuck through the back of her tank top like two oyster shells.

Sweetie and I had a bit of a growler when we got back home. I suggested there had been a conspiracy between her and that human flat tire on the eighth floor. Calling her honesty into question, I challenged her fraudulent description of the piano by invoking the name of the late Grace McDaniels,

one of the most revered sideshow freaks of the twentieth century: "She billed herself as the 'Mule-Faced Woman,'" I
ranted, "not the 'Lady Who Ain't the Cutest Thing in Town.'
It's called truth in advertising! Not only that, her son was her
business manager *and* her valet!"

"What's your point?" Lorrie challenged me.

Realizing my point had skidded off the rails, I told her:
"You have to go down there and tell that pterodactyl you
don't want the fucking thing."

"Fuck you. You go tell her," she responded.

"This was your little scheme, not mine. You knew what
you were doing. I'm the victim here."

"You're insane."

Sore spot.

"I knew that was coming! That's always your cheap little
go-to . . . uh . . . what the fuck is it called . . . your little
smart-bomb thing . . . your big scene-stealer whenever you
know I'm right and you're—"

The front door slammed. The Kid was home from school.
She ran into the living room and threw her arms around my
waist.

"Did you see the piano, Daddy? Isn't it beautiful?"

The day the porters wheeled the piano into my apartment, I realized this was something much more than just a large
grotesque object entering my home. A gust of air smacked me

in the face as it rolled by, announcing the stench of other lives: the musk of triumphs and failures, faith and doubt, shitty diapers and cremation urns. As if I didn't have enough on my plate. But I let it go. I did it for my darling daughter. Gagging down a teaspoon of false optimism, I thought if anyone on earth could coax something new and beautiful out of that cigar crate, it would be her. Maybe the Resnick curse had skipped a generation.

The Kid threw herself into piano lessons. The notes that initially lumbered through the apartment may have been sour and uncivilized, but at least they were loud and plentiful. As the weeks passed, my ears, admittedly untrained, could detect no improvement. To be perfectly honest, I think she was getting worse. Soon, grievances were lodged—the Kid wasn't thrilled with the songs the Hot Asian Chick was teaching her. She didn't give a shit about the girl with the lamb or the bridge collapse in London; she wanted to pound out the stuff she heard in the Charlie Brown cartoons. *The apple don't fall far from the tree,* I proudly thought. On week eleven, she officially quit. I'll never forget that day as long as I live: the piano teacher was wearing a halter top. Lorrie and I had a gentle talk with the Kid about the concept of patience, but she wouldn't be swayed. She informed us she was giving up on music and sticking with television, an instrument she'd already mastered. The Resnick curse was alive and kicking. A few days later, while goofing around with friends, she knocked over a container of turtle food, scattering thousands of compressed shrimp pellets all over the piano. The tiny particles wedged themselves between the keys and resisted the best efforts of a vacuum cleaner. Subsequently, any attempt at playing the chromatic scale was accompanied by what sounded like a pepper grinder (something the digital keyboard could do in its sleep). Soon the entire apartment smelled like a dumpster behind Panda Express, and Lorrie offered little opposition when I announced the piano had to go. The turtle, which now enjoyed strolling across the keyboard, pecking for treasure, didn't get a vote.

The "!!!FREE PIANO!!! (NEEDS A LITTLE TLC)" listing ran on Craigslist for thirty days. In the spirit of self-flagellation, I relisted it for another thirty days. A friend of a friend briefly expressed interest, but his wife's allergy to shellfish queered the deal. It was like trying to give away donuts in a graveyard (to borrow another phrase from my deeply disturbed shop teacher). Once the Kid realized we were really, *really* trying to ditch the thing, she had a change of heart: "How could you get rid of my piano?" she moaned. "I *love* that piano! I want to keep it forever!" Then she turned on the old sprinkler system and I looked for a gun to put in my mouth.

The piano had become a boarder in the apartment—one

who was decomposing and fucking us on the rent. I found myself coming home later and later—anything to avoid being around it. Lorrie and I were fighting more than usual. On some nights, before my meds kicked in, I was convinced that if I lifted the piano lid, I'd find the lady on eight curled up inside it, weeping, "You promised to give it a happy home."

The idea had been gestating, in one form or another, for some time. Finally, I saw an opening. The Kid was invited to visit a friend in the country for a few days over winter break. When she returned, the tale would go like this: Mommy read about a little girl in the newspaper who lived in a homeless shelter. Every night, the little girl kneeled by her rusty cot and prayed to Santa for a piano. But Santa was in a bind: How could he possibly fit a piano on his sled? That's when Mommy got a great idea: What if we gave the little girl *our* piano! "A Christmas Miracle" we'd call it.

I pitched the plan to Lorrie, who'd been looking a bit fatigued of late but remained surprisingly sharp. Her only note was to cut "Mommy" and replace it with "Daddy." I felt it was a juvenile request, but agreed in the spirit of compromise. I embraced her, elated that we were generally on the same page. "That's why we're still in love," I said. "We're always generally on the same page."

There's nothing more delicious than luxuriating in the minutiae of a diabolical plot. How thrilling once the chess pieces start traipsing about the board. My first move, obviously, was the most critical: getting rid of the thing. I mused about chopping it up with a hatchet and taking it down to the river in little pieces. Lorrie, as she's known to do, came up with something a good deal saner. After making a few calls, she learned that the sanitation department, on select days, provided free curbside removal of "large bulky items" such as sofas, appliances, and, one assumes, the odd steel drum containing a state witness. Remarkably, pianos were part of the deal. I was a happy taxpayer.

We waved goodbye to the Kid as the Volvo Cross Country pulled away from the curb and headed north up West End Avenue. She looked so joyful, sitting in the way-back with her little pals, hugging her orange plastic sled. It was one of those wonderful moments when the important things in life suddenly come into sharp focus. Half an hour later, the porters had the piano hog-tied to a dolly and were wheeling it to the freight elevator. A trail of dislodged turtle food ran through our apartment and down the tenth-floor hallway—as if it were dropping breadcrumbs, hoping to find its way home one day. *Nice try, prick. Rot in the dump.*

The sanitation department collected bulk items in the early-morning hours, which meant it would be gone by the time I woke up. After dinner that night, I went outside for a walk. I wanted the satisfaction of seeing it out there, waiting for its ride. With a little luck, maybe a dog would piss on it.

The porters had set the piano on the curb around the corner. It stood alone under a streetlamp, looking resigned and undignified. The bench lay upside down on top of it; its ornamental legs jutted skyward like a dead click beetle. As people walked by, several stopped to acknowledge the instrument, as if recognizing an old friend who'd fallen on hard times. A family toting leftover bags from Carmine's approached it and the husband solemnly remarked, "Well, that's the saddest thing I've ever seen." His little boy patted the key lid and murmured, "Awww." Fearful of a chance look in my direction, I receded into my building's courtyard to observe from the shadows, like an arsonist, returning to witness the blaze he'd set.

Lorrie and I spent the evening peeking down through a crack in the bedroom curtain, watching the parade pass by. People of every color and all walks of life stopped to pay their respects to the piano. There were varying expressions of outrage, compassion, and the somber uncertainty of life. I sensed Lorrie was in a funk, so I offered a different perspective: "People are full of shit. For all this melodrama, not one of 'em seems to want the fucking thing."

She didn't respond. She just gazed down at the street.

Finally, she said, "This was a mistake."

Lorrie was worried that the lady on eight would see it and her heart would be broken. The piano had meant so much to her. It had survived all those decades in her family before briefly coming into our possession, and we junked it.

I understood what she was saying, but all I could really muster was, "Who cares?"

That touched a nerve for some reason and out it poured. She felt I had imposed my will on her, wore her down to get my way. We should've been patient. The piano could've been professionally cleaned. We could've found it a good home. I asked if she meant a farm where it would have lots of room to run around. Her nostrils flared, and she unloaded all the candy—calling me an asshole, a fucking asshole, a fucking jerk, and a pussy. I had a funny response on the tip of my tongue but withheld it in the interest of not getting clocked.

We went to bed in silence. It had been an intense day and I was exhausted. I fell into a deep sleep, occasionally roused by an "accidental" elbow to my temple. (Strangely, these nighttime fender benders had grown more frequent over the years, despite upgrading to a king-size mattress.) I thought about the lady on eight. I had simply been minding my own business when she inserted herself into my life. It was nothing new. The more I try to hide, the more they find me.

The sound of the Kid playing the piano was one of the

most enchanting things I'd ever heard. Lorrie and I stood behind her, arms around each other, watching those little fingers whirl across the keyboard. Through uncontrollable sobs my wife thanked me for having the wisdom and patience to let the Kid revisit her dream when she was ready. She asked me if I could find it within my heart to forgive her. Then she put her hand down my pants.

I stirred awake, but the sound of the piano was still in my head, accompanied by rowdy laughter and shrill voices. It was two a.m. I rose and looked out the window. A band of shit-faced college kids, home for winter break, was gathered around the piano, taking turns at the keyboard. A few of the girls managed to turn out something like a melody, while the guys just banged on the keys like assholes, laughing, as guys often do, at things that aren't funny. I tried to go back to sleep, but for hours it seemed like every student from Oberlin, Wesleyan, and Tufts took their turn at the piano while loudly exchanging such collegiate wordplay as. "Wooo!" or "My turn!" or "Dude, you suck!"

Sometime around four a.m., the street finally fell quiet. But I lay awake, eyes wide open, anticipating the approaching rumble of the garbage truck. I became aware of the sound of my own breathing when I noticed a hint of light outlining the window shade. Had I nodded off and slept through it? Again, I left the bed and peered outside. It was a steady snow. A cab was slowly edging down the street, fishtailing to a stop at the traffic light. The piano stood there undisturbed, white and sparkling under the streetlamp.

The blizzard continued into the next day. Alternate-side parking and garbage collection had been suspended. There would be no bulk pickup. Enrobed in a thick blanket of snow, the piano had taken on the appearance of a lavish cake or a piece of sculpture. People took pictures with their cell phones.

We were low on GoLean Crunch and completely out of milk. I was hungry and climbing the walls—but I couldn't go out, fearing a chance encounter with the lady on eight. Lorrie, also gripped by cabin fever, had curled herself up in a small uncomfortable chair usually favored by the dog. She smiled at me psychotically as she gnawed on a stale Teddy Graham. "Aren't you starving?" I asked, hoping it would compel her to go out and bring back provisions. "No," she replied, in a tranquil voice. "I've got everything I need for the rest of my life." She put another bear in her mouth and swallowed it whole. Lorrie knew I was afraid of what was out there, and she was enjoying it. But I wasn't about to give her the satisfaction. "Well, *I'm* going out to get some food," I said, grabbing my coat and stomping toward the door. "Some *real* food." Then I stopped. Trying to be the bigger man, I gave her another chance: "You sure you don't want to come along, hon? It's pretty out."

"Use your brain."

She was clearly in a mood.

I stood in the elevator, tense and unable to breathe until the indicator safely passed the eighth floor. *This was no way to live,* I thought. The doorman and the porters were in the middle of a hushed conversation as I stepped into the lobby. They immediately clammed up.

"Looks like we got us a little snow out there, gentlemen," I said in my best jovial, full-of-shit voice. Gabriel, the doorman, normally deliriously chatty on the topic of weather, just cocked his head toward the big glass doors and muttered flatly, "As you see." The porters turned away, trying not to make eye contact. I caught a glimpse of the security monitor that sat on the front desk. A grainy black-and-white image of the snow-covered piano flickered in the upper right quadrant. It was striking and perfectly framed, as if Orson Welles had composed it for a dream sequence. Gabriel noticed me staring at it.

"Is pretty, right?" he said.

I pretended I didn't hear him.

"Yeah, a lot of people say they would've taken it. Miss Orbach—4A—she told me she would've taken it."

"Well, I don't know Miss Orbach," I grunted.

"She said maybe you should've put up a flyer by the mailboxes."

"Tell her she's welcome to towel it off."

My instincts had been correct: by now, everyone on the West Side knew I was the monster who threw out the piano. The mob was already lighting their torches. By nightfall I'd be chased through the Ramble in Central Park before they'd have me trapped in Belvedere Castle. The last thing I'd see from the blazing tower would be Lorrie, cheering along with the crowd, as she shared a Teddy Graham with the lady on eight. I returned to the elevator. Venturing outside at this time seemed ill-advised.

It was another day and a half before the streets were cleared and sanitation services resumed. By then, the piano was waterlogged and noticeably sagging. No one tried to play it anymore. No one took pictures.

In the predawn twilight of a cool January morning, I awoke to a tremendous noise rising up from Eighty-first Street. It sounded like a tigress taking down an impala—a convulsive din of crunching and groaning, splintering wood, and the startled yip of snapping wires. Lorrie's head rose briefly. She glared at me and then rolled to her other side.

The Kid returned the next day and I was truthful; I told her everything. Her face slowly contorted, and then the levee blew. I held her tight and apologized over and over, I told her how much I loved her, I offered to buy her another turtle and tossed in a water frog. She took the deal, but deep down, I knew we weren't square. It was a betrayal. A scar. It was the my-father-got-rid-of-my-piano story; something she'd share one day with her college roommates, her husband, her children, and her psychiatrist. It would earn a few crucial frames in her final reel of memories and travel with her into the next life. When it comes to the bad stuff, there's nothing too small that's not worth dwelling on forever. I say, anyway.

I was making my way down the narrow staircase at Fairway Market, holding a box of herbal tea that's supposed to make you smart. She was on her way up. I didn't recognize her. Her hair was done—blown straight or something—and she wore a belted, blue-purplish coat that you could almost call stylish. She looked younger. I managed a clumsy smile as I tried to squeeze by. She took hold of my arm, and that's when I actually saw her.

"I'm so sorry the piano didn't work out," the lady on eight said. "I'm just happy your daughter got to enjoy it for a while."

I started to lose my balance and almost fell down the stairs, but she had a firm hold on my wrist.

"Well, you know kids," I replied, as if reciting a line in a play, "they want one thing one minute and something else the next."

"Oh, I understand," she said with a laugh. "It's not your fault."

"We really tried to find it a home," I went on, "but it just took up so much room and my mother's coming for a visit and she's not feeling well, so . . ."

She smiled and nodded and seemed to be counting the number of times my eyes blinked. Then she wished my mother well and said she had to run; she was picking up a few things before catching a flight out west to shoot a Lanacane commercial. "That was a lucky one," she said. "It just fell out of the air." Then she floated away.

About the Author

Adam Resnick is an Emmy Award–winning writer who began his career at *Late Night with David Letterman*. He went on to cocreate the Fox sitcom, *Get a Life*, and has written several screenplays, including cult favorites *Cabin Boy* and *Death to Smoochy*. Resnick has written for *Saturday Night Live*, was a co-executive producer and writer for HBO's *The Larry Sanders Show*, and created the HBO series *The High Life*, which was produced by David Letterman's company, Worldwide Pants. He lives in New York City.